TEST PREP WORKBOOK

SIDE by SIDE

1

Plus

Steven J. Molinsky • Bill Bliss

Side by Side Plus Test Prep Workbook 1

Pearson Education, 10 Bank Street, White Plains, NY 10606

Staff credits: The people who make up the *Side by Side Plus* team, representing content creation, design, manufacturing, marketing, multimedia, project management, publishing, rights management, and testing are Pietro Alongi, Allen Ascher, Rhea Banker, Elizabeth Barker, Lisa Bayrasli, Elizabeth Carlson, Jennifer Castro, Tracey Munz Cataldo, Diane Cipollone, Aerin Csigay, Victoria Denkus, Dave Dickey, Daniel Dwyer, Wanda España, Oliva Fernandez, Warren Fischbach, Pam Fishman, Nancy Flaggman, Patrice Fraccio, Irene Frankel, Aliza Greenblatt, Lester Holmes, Janet Johnston, Caroline Kasterine, Barry Katzen, Ray Keating, Renee Langan, Jaime Lieber, José Antonio Méndez, Julie Molnar, Alison Pei, Pamela Pia, Stuart Radcliffe, Jennifer Raspiller, Kriston Reinmuth, Mary Perrotta Rich, Tania Saiz-Sousa, Katherine Sullivan, Paula Van Ells, Kenneth Volcjak, Paula Williams, and Wendy Wolf.

Text composition: TSI Graphics, Inc.

Illustrations: Richard E. Hill

The authors gratefully acknowledge the contribution of Tina Carver in the development of the original *Side by Side* program.

ISBN-10: 0-13-418677-X
ISBN-13: 978-0-13-418677-1

Printed in the United States of America

1 2 3 4 5 6 7 8 9 10—V011—22 21 20 19 18 17 16 15

CONTENTS

PREFACE

Side by Side Plus Test Prep Workbook 1 provides unit achievement tests designed to reinforce and assess the learning objectives in *Side by Side Plus Student Book 1*. The tests provide focused coverage of lifeskill competencies and employment topics, assess student progress, and prepare students for the types of standardized tests and performance assessments used by many instructional programs. The content of each test is based on the grammar, vocabulary, and topics covered in the particular unit of the student book.

The achievement tests offer students practice with a variety of test-item formats:

- Multiple-choice questions assess vocabulary, grammar, reading, lifeskill and work-related competencies, and literacy tasks (such as reading medicine labels and filling out forms).
- Listening assessments offer practice with the types of listening comprehension tasks common in standardized tests.
- Writing assessments can be evaluated using a scoring rubric and collected in portfolios of students' work.
- Speaking performance assessments are designed to stimulate face-to-face interactions between students, for evaluation by the teacher using a standardized scoring rubric, or for self-evaluation by students. (The speaking assessments can also be used to evaluate students individually if time and resources allow for teachers or aides to conduct these assessments on a one-to-one basis.)

Test pages are perforated so that completed tests can be handed in and can serve as a record of students' participation and progress in the instructional program.

The Digital Audio CD included with the Workbook contains all listening activities in the achievement tests. You may choose to do these activities in class or have students complete them on their own using the audio. Listening scripts are provided in *Side by Side Plus Teacher's Guide 1*.

Side by Side Plus Multilevel Activity & Achievement Test Book 1 (included with the Teacher's Guide) provides test preparation strategies, answer keys, scoring rubrics, and resources for documenting students' progress—all in a volume of reproducible masters and an accompanying CD-ROM.

Name _____

Date _____ **Class** _____

A PERSONAL INFORMATION & FORMS

Name: (1) _____

Street: (2) _____ Apartment: (3) _____

City: (4) _____ State: (5) _____ Zip Code: (6) _____

Telephone: (7) _____ E-Mail: (8) _____ Age: (9) _____

Social Security Number: (10) _____ Country of Origin: (11) _____

Look at the information. Choose the correct line on the form.

Example:

062-41-9275

- Ⓐ Line 2
- Ⓑ Line 3
- Ⓒ Line 9
- Ⓓ Line 10   Ⓐ Ⓑ Ⓒ ●

1. Mexico

- Ⓐ Line 1
- Ⓑ Line 6
- Ⓒ Line 8
- Ⓓ Line 11

2. Los Angeles

- Ⓐ Line 2
- Ⓑ Line 3
- Ⓒ Line 4
- Ⓓ Line 7

3. 6-A

- Ⓐ Line 3
- Ⓑ Line 6
- Ⓒ Line 9
- Ⓓ Line 10

4. 90021

- Ⓐ Line 2
- Ⓑ Line 6
- Ⓒ Line 7
- Ⓓ Line 9

5. 840 Central Avenue

- Ⓐ Line 1
- Ⓑ Line 2
- Ⓒ Line 4
- Ⓓ Line 8

. . . .

1 Ⓐ Ⓑ Ⓒ Ⓓ   3 Ⓐ Ⓑ Ⓒ Ⓓ   5 Ⓐ Ⓑ Ⓒ Ⓓ

2 Ⓐ Ⓑ Ⓒ Ⓓ   4 Ⓐ Ⓑ Ⓒ Ⓓ

Go to the next page ⟩   **1** ●

B INFORMATION ON AN ENVELOPE

Sally Grant
360 Lake Street, Apt. 4-D
Los Angeles, California 90016

Choose the correct answer.

Example:

last name
- Ⓐ Sally
- Ⓑ Lake
- Ⓒ Grant
- Ⓓ Los Angeles   Ⓐ Ⓑ ● Ⓓ

6. state
- Ⓐ Street
- Ⓑ Grant
- Ⓒ Los Angeles
- Ⓓ California

7. first name
- Ⓐ Lake
- Ⓑ Sally
- Ⓒ Grant
- Ⓓ Street

8. address
- Ⓐ 360 Lake Street
- Ⓑ Sally Grant
- Ⓒ 90016
- Ⓓ California

9. apartment number
- Ⓐ 360
- Ⓑ 4-D
- Ⓒ 90016
- Ⓓ 4

10. city
- Ⓐ California
- Ⓑ Grant
- Ⓒ Lake Street
- Ⓓ Los Angeles

C COMMON ABBREVIATIONS IN ADDRESSES

Look at the abbreviation. Choose the correct answer.

Example:

W.
- Ⓐ East
- Ⓑ West
- Ⓒ North
- Ⓓ South   Ⓐ ● Ⓒ Ⓓ

11. N.
- Ⓐ East
- Ⓑ West
- Ⓒ North
- Ⓓ South

12. Ave.
- Ⓐ Apartment
- Ⓑ Avenue
- Ⓒ Street
- Ⓓ East

13. St.
- Ⓐ South
- Ⓑ West
- Ⓒ Street
- Ⓓ East

· ·

6 Ⓐ Ⓑ Ⓒ Ⓓ   8 Ⓐ Ⓑ Ⓒ Ⓓ   10 Ⓐ Ⓑ Ⓒ Ⓓ   12 Ⓐ Ⓑ Ⓒ Ⓓ

7 Ⓐ Ⓑ Ⓒ Ⓓ   9 Ⓐ Ⓑ Ⓒ Ⓓ   11 Ⓐ Ⓑ Ⓒ Ⓓ   13 Ⓐ Ⓑ Ⓒ Ⓓ

Go to the next page ⟩

Name _____   Date _____

D GRAMMAR IN CONTEXT: Asking About & Giving Personal Information

Choose the correct answer to complete the conversation.

Example:
What's your _____?
- (A) address
- ● name
- (C) city
- (D) state

My name is David Chen.

14. What's your _____?
- (A) name
- (B) city
- (C) state
- (D) address

427 Central Street.

15. What's your _____?
- (A) address
- (B) phone number
- (C) social security number
- (D) apartment number

963-2434.

16. _____ are you from?
- (A) What's
- (B) What's your
- (C) Where
- (D) Where are

I'm from China.

17. _____ do you spell your last name?
- (A) How
- (B) Where
- (C) What's
- (D) Who

C–H–E–N.

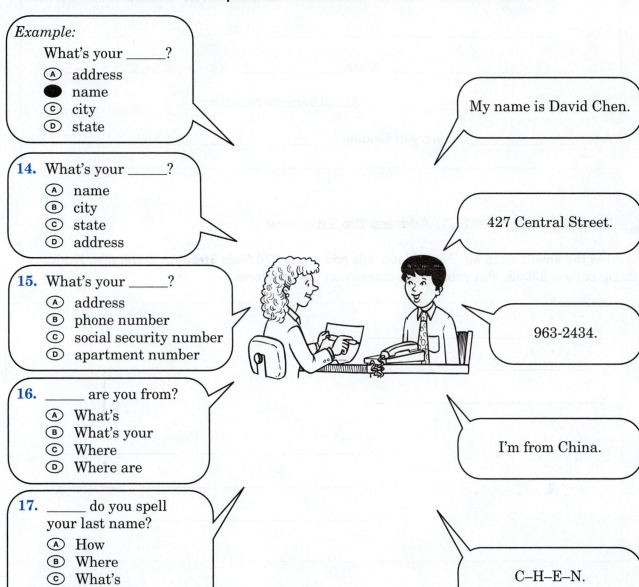

E LISTENING ASSESSMENT

Read and listen to the questions. Then listen to the interview, and answer the questions.

18. What's her last name?
- (A) Sally
- (B) Susan
- (C) Keller
- (D) Geller

19. What's her phone number?
- (A) 68 Central Avenue
- (B) 86 Central Avenue
- (C) 681-2394
- (D) 861-2394

20. What's her address?
- (A) 68 Central Avenue
- (B) 86 Central Avenue
- (C) 681-2394
- (D) 861-2394

. . . .

14 (A) (B) (C) (D)   16 (A) (B) (C) (D)   18 (A) (B) (C) (D)   20 (A) (B) (C) (D)

15 (A) (B) (C) (D)   17 (A) (B) (C) (D)   19 (A) (B) (C) (D)

F WRITING ASSESSMENT: Fill Out the Form

Name: _____

Street: _____ Apartment: _____

City: _____ State: _____ Zip Code: _____

Telephone: _____ Social Security Number: _____

Age: _____ Country of Origin: _____

G WRITING ASSESSMENT: Address the Envelope

**Address the envelope to Mr. Peter Black. His address is 378 Main Street in Waterville, Florida.
His zip code is 33068. Put your return address on the envelope.**

_____

_____

_____

                                   _____

                                   _____

                                   _____

H SPEAKING ASSESSMENT

I can ask and answer these questions:

Ask Answer

☐ ☐ What's your name?
☐ ☐ What's your address?
☐ ☐ What's your telephone number?
☐ ☐ What's your social security number?
☐ ☐ What's your age?
☐ ☐ Where are you from?

Ask Answer

☐ ☐ Who is the president of the United States?
☐ ☐ Who is the president or prime minister of your native country?
☐ ☐ Who is the mayor of our city?
☐ ☐ Who is the governor of our state?

STOP

Name ______________________

Date ______________ Class ______________

2

A CLASSROOM ITEMS & SIMPLE COMMANDS

Choose the correct answer.

Example:

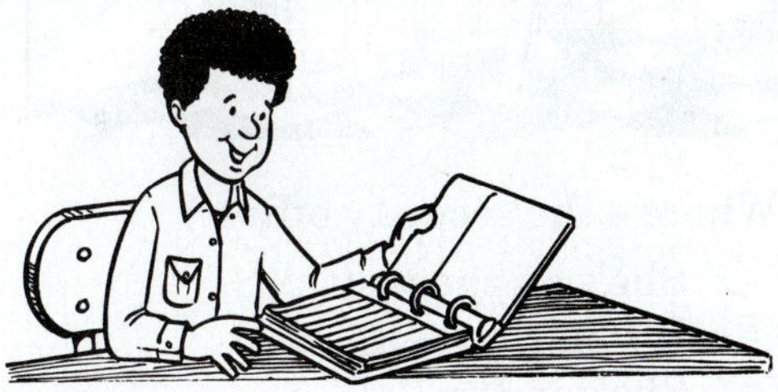

Open your _____.

- Ⓐ chair
- Ⓑ desk
- Ⓒ book
- ● notebook

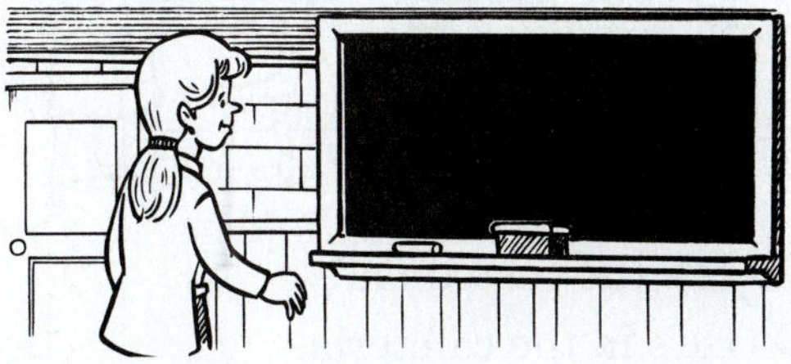

1. Go to the _____.

- Ⓐ book
- Ⓑ bookshelf
- Ⓒ board
- Ⓓ globe

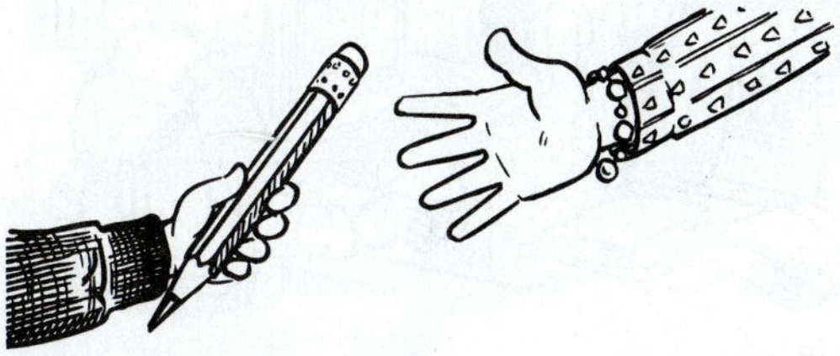

2. Give me the _____.

- Ⓐ ruler
- Ⓑ pencil
- Ⓒ clock
- Ⓓ wall

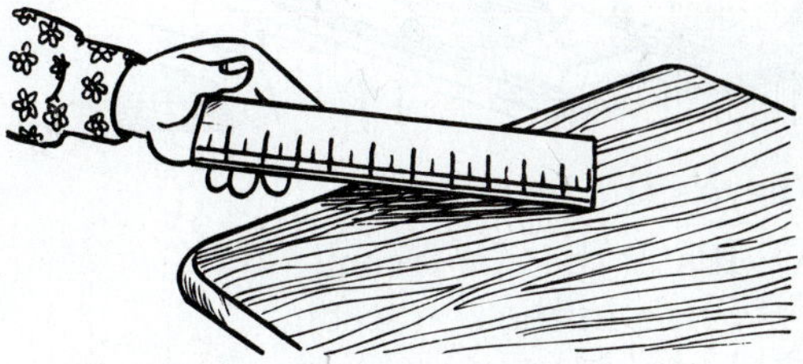

3. Put the _____ on the desk.

- Ⓐ dictionary
- Ⓑ computer
- Ⓒ pen
- Ⓓ ruler

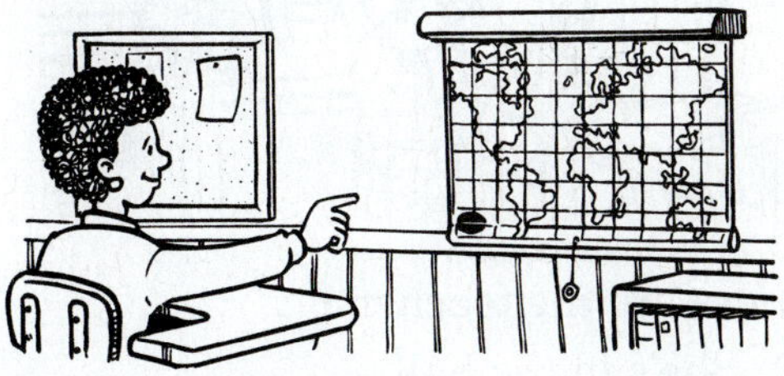

4. Point to the _____.

- Ⓐ table
- Ⓑ map
- Ⓒ globe
- Ⓓ bulletin board

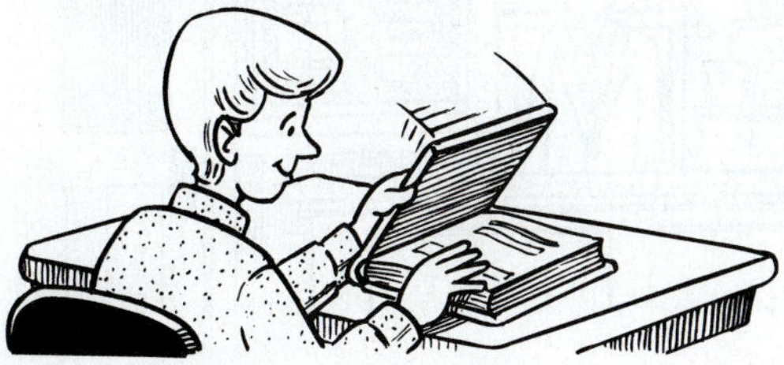

5. Close your _____.

- Ⓐ book
- Ⓑ wall
- Ⓒ table
- Ⓓ pen

1 Ⓐ Ⓑ Ⓒ Ⓓ	3 Ⓐ Ⓑ Ⓒ Ⓓ	5 Ⓐ Ⓑ Ⓒ Ⓓ
2 Ⓐ Ⓑ Ⓒ Ⓓ	4 Ⓐ Ⓑ Ⓒ Ⓓ	

Go to the next page

Choose the correct answer.

Example:

Where's the principal?

Ⓐ It's in the classroom.
Ⓑ She's in the classroom.
Ⓒ He's in the principal's office.
● She's in the principal's office.

6. Where are the teachers?

Ⓐ She's in the hall.
Ⓑ They're in the hall.
Ⓒ He's in the classroom.
Ⓓ They're in the classroom.

7. Where's the clerk?

Ⓐ They're in the classroom.
Ⓑ It's on the desk.
Ⓒ She's in the hall.
Ⓓ He's in the office.

8. Where's the security officer?

Ⓐ She's on the wall.
Ⓑ It's on the wall.
Ⓒ She's in the hall.
Ⓓ It's in the hall.

9. Where's the custodian?

Ⓐ He's in the cafeteria.
Ⓑ He's in the classroom.
Ⓒ He's in the hall.
Ⓓ He's in the office.

10. Where's the librarian?

Ⓐ She's in the bookshelf.
Ⓑ She's in the library.
Ⓒ It's in the school.
Ⓓ She's in the hospital.

. . . .

6 Ⓐ Ⓑ Ⓒ Ⓓ   8 Ⓐ Ⓑ Ⓒ Ⓓ   10 Ⓐ Ⓑ Ⓒ Ⓓ

7 Ⓐ Ⓑ Ⓒ Ⓓ   9 Ⓐ Ⓑ Ⓒ Ⓓ

Go to the next page ▷

C **GRAMMAR IN CONTEXT: Greeting • Locating Classroom Items**

Choose the correct answer to complete the conversation.

Example:
Hi. _____
- Ⓐ Fine.
- Ⓑ Fine, thanks.
- Ⓒ And you?
- ⬤ How are you?

11. _____
- Ⓐ Bye.
- Ⓑ Goodbye.
- Ⓒ Fine. And you?
- Ⓓ How are you?

12. _____ the pencils?
- Ⓐ Where's
- Ⓑ What's
- Ⓒ What are
- Ⓓ Where are

13. _____ on the desk.
- Ⓐ They're
- Ⓑ I'm
- Ⓒ We're
- Ⓓ It's

14. Where's the _____?
- Ⓐ clock
- Ⓑ computer
- Ⓒ dictionary
- Ⓓ ruler

15. The monitor and the _____ are on the table.
- Ⓐ board
- Ⓑ notebook
- Ⓒ keyboard
- Ⓓ bulletin board

16. _____ the CD?
- Ⓐ What's
- Ⓑ Where's
- Ⓒ What are
- Ⓓ Where are

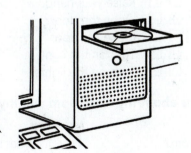

17. It's in the _____.
- Ⓐ dictionary
- Ⓑ keyboard
- Ⓒ disk drive
- Ⓓ desk

· ·

11 Ⓐ Ⓑ Ⓒ Ⓓ   13 Ⓐ Ⓑ Ⓒ Ⓓ   15 Ⓐ Ⓑ Ⓒ Ⓓ   17 Ⓐ Ⓑ Ⓒ Ⓓ

12 Ⓐ Ⓑ Ⓒ Ⓓ   14 Ⓐ Ⓑ Ⓒ Ⓓ   16 Ⓐ Ⓑ Ⓒ Ⓓ

Go to the next page ⟹

Read and listen to the questions. Then listen to the conversation, and answer the questions.

18. What's the principal's name?
- Ⓐ Rosa.
- Ⓑ Mr. Wilson.
- Ⓒ Mr. Lane.
- Ⓓ Mrs. Lane.

19. Where's the teacher?
- Ⓐ He's in the hospital.
- Ⓑ He's in the classroom.
- Ⓒ He's at the dentist.
- Ⓓ He's the principal.

20. Which student is absent today?
- Ⓐ Mr. Wilson.
- Ⓑ Rosa.
- Ⓒ Mrs. Wilson.
- Ⓓ Mrs. Lane.

E WRITING ASSESSMENT: Classroom Objects

Write about the objects in your classroom. What are they, and where are they?

....

....

....

F WRITING ASSESSMENT: School Personnel

Write about the people in your school — your teacher, the principal, the security guard, and other people. What are their names? Where are they now?

....

....

....

....

G SPEAKING ASSESSMENT

I can give and respond to these commands:

Give	Respond	
☐	☐	Stand up.
☐	☐	Go to the board.
☐	☐	Write your name.
☐	☐	Erase your name.
☐	☐	Sit down.

Give	Respond	
☐	☐	Raise your hand.
☐	☐	Open the door.
☐	☐	Close the door.
☐	☐	Turn on the lights.
☐	☐	Turn off the lights.

Give	Respond	
☐	☐	Open your book.
☐	☐	Close your book.
☐	☐	Give me a pen/pencil.
☐	☐	Point to the door.
☐	☐	Point to the board.

I can ask and answer these questions about my classroom and my school:

Ask	Answer	
☐	☐	What objects are in our classroom?
☐	☐	Where's the _object_ ?
☐	☐	What's on your desk?

Ask	Answer	
☐	☐	What's our teacher's name?
☐	☐	What's the principal's name?
☐	☐	Where's the principal?

• •

18 Ⓐ Ⓑ Ⓒ Ⓓ   **19** Ⓐ Ⓑ Ⓒ Ⓓ   **20** Ⓐ Ⓑ Ⓒ Ⓓ

STOP

Name _____

Date _____ Class _____

3

A COMMON CLASSROOM & HOME ACTIVITIES

Choose the correct answer.

Example:

What's Ms. Jenner doing?
- (A) She's reading.
- (B) He's cooking.
- (C) She's cooking.
- ● She's eating.

1. What's Mr. Gray doing?

- (A) He's studying.
- (B) She's watching TV.
- (C) He's watching TV.
- (D) He's playing cards.

2. What's Miss Lewis doing?

- (A) She's reading.
- (B) I'm reading.
- (C) He's reading.
- (D) It's reading.

3. What are your friends doing?

- (A) He's playing the guitar.
- (B) They're playing the guitar.
- (C) She's playing baseball.
- (D) They're playing baseball.

4. What's your dog doing?
- (A) I'm sleeping.
- (B) It's sleeping.
- (C) We're sleeping.
- (D) They're sleeping.

5. What are you and Carla doing?
- (A) I'm studying English.
- (B) They're studying English.
- (C) We're studying English.
- (D) She's studying English.

6. What's Mrs. Carter doing?

- (A) He's teaching.
- (B) She's teaching.
- (C) He's playing.
- (D) She's planting.

7. What's Jimmy doing?
- (A) He's playing the piano.
- (B) He's playing baseball.
- (C) He's playing with the dog.
- (D) He's playing the guitar.

8. What are Mr. and Mrs. Lu doing?
- (A) We're eating.
- (B) They're eating.
- (C) They're cooking.
- (D) We're cooking.

9. What are the students doing?
- (A) They're studying English.
- (B) We're studying English.
- (C) I'm studying mathematics.
- (D) He's studying mathematics.

10. What am I doing?

- (A) She's reading a book.
- (B) He's reading the newspaper.
- (C) You're reading a book.
- (D) I'm reading the newspaper.

11. What are your friends doing?
- (A) We're singing.
- (B) You're singing.
- (C) I'm singing.
- (D) They're singing.

· ·

1 (A) (B) (C) (D)   4 (A) (B) (C) (D)   7 (A) (B) (C) (D)   10 (A) (B) (C) (D)

2 (A) (B) (C) (D)   5 (A) (B) (C) (D)   8 (A) (B) (C) (D)   11 (A) (B) (C) (D)

3 (A) (B) (C) (D)   6 (A) (B) (C) (D)   9 (A) (B) (C) (D)

Go to the next page →

9

B GRAMMAR IN CONTEXT: Asking About Home Activities • Checking Understanding

Choose the correct answer to complete the conversation.

12. Where are _____?
- Ⓐ I
- Ⓑ she
- Ⓒ he
- Ⓓ you

13. _____ in the kitchen.
- Ⓐ I'm
- Ⓑ She's
- Ⓒ They're
- Ⓓ It's

14. In the _____?
- Ⓐ hospital
- Ⓑ park
- Ⓒ kitchen
- Ⓓ classroom

15. Yes. I'm _____.
- Ⓐ kitchen
- Ⓑ in the kitchen
- Ⓒ the kitchen
- Ⓓ doing

16. What _____ you doing?
- Ⓐ am
- Ⓑ are
- Ⓒ is
- Ⓓ I

17. _____ cooking.
- Ⓐ You're
- Ⓑ They're
- Ⓒ I'm
- Ⓓ She's

C LISTENING ASSESSMENT

Read and listen to the questions. Then listen to the story, and answer the questions.

18. What are Mr. and Mrs. Baker doing?
- Ⓐ They're eating.
- Ⓑ They're swimming.
- Ⓒ He's reading.
- Ⓓ They're reading.

19. What's Tommy doing?
- Ⓐ He's swimming.
- Ⓑ He's reading.
- Ⓒ He's listening to music.
- Ⓓ She's listening to music.

20. Where are they today?
- Ⓐ It's a beautiful day.
- Ⓑ They're very happy.
- Ⓒ They're at home.
- Ⓓ They're at the beach.

D WRITING ASSESSMENT

What are you doing now? What are your friends doing?

....

....

E SPEAKING ASSESSMENT

I can ask and answer these questions:

Ask Answer
- ☐ ☐ Where are you?
- ☐ ☐ What are you doing?

Ask Answer
- ☐ ☐ What are other students doing?
- ☐ ☐ What are your friends doing?

12	Ⓐ Ⓑ Ⓒ Ⓓ	15	Ⓐ Ⓑ Ⓒ Ⓓ	18	Ⓐ Ⓑ Ⓒ Ⓓ
13	Ⓐ Ⓑ Ⓒ Ⓓ	16	Ⓐ Ⓑ Ⓒ Ⓓ	19	Ⓐ Ⓑ Ⓒ Ⓓ
14	Ⓐ Ⓑ Ⓒ Ⓓ	17	Ⓐ Ⓑ Ⓒ Ⓓ	20	Ⓐ Ⓑ Ⓒ Ⓓ

STOP

4

A COMMON CLASSROOM & HOME ACTIVITIES

Choose the best answer.

Example:

He's brushing _____ teeth.
- (A) my
- (B) our
- (C) his
- (D) your   Ⓐ Ⓑ ● Ⓓ

1. She's doing _____ homework.
   - (A) my
   - (B) its
   - (C) our
   - (D) her

2. They're opening _____ books.
   - (A) my
   - (B) their
   - (C) her
   - (D) his

3. I'm brushing _____ teeth.
   - (A) their
   - (B) my
   - (C) its
   - (D) his

4. He's raising _____ hand.
   - (A) our
   - (B) her
   - (C) his
   - (D) their

5. We're doing _____ exercises.
   - (A) our
   - (B) their
   - (C) his
   - (D) her

6. What's Mr. Sharp doing?
   - (A) She's cleaning her kitchen.
   - (B) We're cleaning our kitchen.
   - (C) He's cleaning his kitchen.
   - (D) I'm cleaning my kitchen.

7. What are Mr. and Mrs. Lee doing?
   - (A) He's washing his car.
   - (B) She's washing her car.
   - (C) We're washing our car.
   - (D) They're washing their car.

8. Is Ms. Harris busy?
   - (A) Yes, he is.
   - (B) Yes, I am.
   - (C) Yes, she is.
   - (D) Yes, it is.

9. Are you busy?
   - (A) Yes, you are.
   - (B) Yes, I am.
   - (C) Yes, they are.
   - (D) Yes, it is.

10. Are the students studying?
    - (A) Yes, they are.
    - (B) Yes, you are.
    - (C) Yes, I am.
    - (D) Yes, he is.

11. What are your friends doing?
    - (A) We're painting our apartment.
    - (B) She's painting her apartment.
    - (C) I'm painting my apartment.
    - (D) They're painting their apartment.

· ·

1 Ⓐ Ⓑ Ⓒ Ⓓ   4 Ⓐ Ⓑ Ⓒ Ⓓ   7 Ⓐ Ⓑ Ⓒ Ⓓ   10 Ⓐ Ⓑ Ⓒ Ⓓ

2 Ⓐ Ⓑ Ⓒ Ⓓ   5 Ⓐ Ⓑ Ⓒ Ⓓ   8 Ⓐ Ⓑ Ⓒ Ⓓ   11 Ⓐ Ⓑ Ⓒ Ⓓ

3 Ⓐ Ⓑ Ⓒ Ⓓ   6 Ⓐ Ⓑ Ⓒ Ⓓ   9 Ⓐ Ⓑ Ⓒ Ⓓ

Go to the next page ▷

B GRAMMAR IN CONTEXT: Getting Someone's Attention • Asking About Home Activities

Choose the correct answer to complete the conversation.

12. Excuse me. Alex?
_____ you busy?
- Ⓐ Am
- Ⓑ Is
- Ⓒ Are
- Ⓓ I

13. Yes, _____.
- Ⓐ we are
- Ⓑ they are
- Ⓒ he is
- Ⓓ I am

14. What _____ doing?
- Ⓐ are they
- Ⓑ are you
- Ⓒ am I
- Ⓓ is she

15. I'm _____.
- Ⓐ doing their homework
- Ⓑ doing its exercises
- Ⓒ doing my homework
- Ⓓ doing their exercises

16. _____ Bob doing?
- Ⓐ What
- Ⓑ What are
- Ⓒ Where's
- Ⓓ What's

17. _____ washing _____ car.
- Ⓐ He's . . his
- Ⓑ They're . . their
- Ⓒ We're . . our
- Ⓓ I'm . . my

C LISTENING ASSESSMENT

Read and listen to the questions. Then listen to the telephone conversation, and answer the questions.

18. What's Lisa doing?
- Ⓐ She's washing her car.
- Ⓑ She's washing her cat.
- Ⓒ She's watching her windows.
- Ⓓ She's washing her windows.

19. What's Richard doing?
- Ⓐ He's doing his homework.
- Ⓑ He's cooking breakfast.
- Ⓒ He's cooking dinner.
- Ⓓ He's cooking lunch.

20. What are the children doing?
- Ⓐ They're cooking.
- Ⓑ They're doing their exercises.
- Ⓒ They're cleaning.
- Ⓓ They're doing their homework.

D LEARNING SKILL ASSESSMENT: Alphabetizing

Alphabetize the list of names. Write the names in alphabetical (ABC) order.

Molina   _Chang_

Chang   _____

Williams   _____

Lopez   _____

Gomez   _____

E WRITING ASSESSMENT

Write a paragraph about the picture on page 31 of *Side by Side* Book 1. What are the people doing? (Use a separate sheet of paper.)

F SPEAKING ASSESSMENT

I can ask and answer these questions:

Ask Answer
- ☐ ☐ Are you busy?
- ☐ ☐ What are you doing now?
- ☐ ☐ What are your neighbors doing?

12 Ⓐ Ⓑ Ⓒ Ⓓ   15 Ⓐ Ⓑ Ⓒ Ⓓ   18 Ⓐ Ⓑ Ⓒ Ⓓ

13 Ⓐ Ⓑ Ⓒ Ⓓ   16 Ⓐ Ⓑ Ⓒ Ⓓ   19 Ⓐ Ⓑ Ⓒ Ⓓ

14 Ⓐ Ⓑ Ⓒ Ⓓ   17 Ⓐ Ⓑ Ⓒ Ⓓ   20 Ⓐ Ⓑ Ⓒ Ⓓ

STOP

A DESCRIBING PEOPLE, THINGS, & WEATHER

Choose the best answer.

Example:

Is his car new or _____?

Ⓐ small
Ⓑ easy
Ⓒ old
Ⓓ thin   Ⓐ Ⓑ ● Ⓓ

1. Is her dog big or _____?

   Ⓐ new
   Ⓑ difficult
   Ⓒ noisy
   Ⓓ little

2. Is your brother single or _____?

   Ⓐ tall
   Ⓑ married
   Ⓒ young
   Ⓓ old

3. Are your neighbors quiet or _____?

   Ⓐ noisy
   Ⓑ cheap
   Ⓒ large
   Ⓓ expensive

4. Is your computer old or _____?

   Ⓐ small
   Ⓑ young
   Ⓒ new
   Ⓓ pretty

5. Is it sunny or _____?

   Ⓐ cold
   Ⓑ cloudy
   Ⓒ cool
   Ⓓ hot

6. _____ is pretty.

   Ⓐ Jill cat
   Ⓑ Cat Jill
   Ⓒ Jill's cat
   Ⓓ Jill's cats

7. _____ is large.

   Ⓐ Mr. Grant's car's
   Ⓑ Mr. Grant's cars
   Ⓒ Mr. Grant car
   Ⓓ Mr. Grant's car

8. The questions in our book _____.

   Ⓐ is difficult
   Ⓑ are difficult
   Ⓒ am difficult
   Ⓓ not difficult

9. Is it raining?

   Ⓐ Yes, he is.
   Ⓑ Yes, I am.
   Ⓒ No, it isn't.
   Ⓓ No, we aren't.

10. Are you married?

    Ⓐ No, you aren't.
    Ⓑ No, they aren't.
    Ⓒ No, he isn't.
    Ⓓ No, I'm not.

11. How's the weather?

    Ⓐ It's cool.
    Ⓑ It's cheap.
    Ⓒ It's short.
    Ⓓ It's thin.

1 Ⓐ Ⓑ Ⓒ Ⓓ   4 Ⓐ Ⓑ Ⓒ Ⓓ   7 Ⓐ Ⓑ Ⓒ Ⓓ   10 Ⓐ Ⓑ Ⓒ Ⓓ

2 Ⓐ Ⓑ Ⓒ Ⓓ   5 Ⓐ Ⓑ Ⓒ Ⓓ   8 Ⓐ Ⓑ Ⓒ Ⓓ   11 Ⓐ Ⓑ Ⓒ Ⓓ

3 Ⓐ Ⓑ Ⓒ Ⓓ   6 Ⓐ Ⓑ Ⓒ Ⓓ   9 Ⓐ Ⓑ Ⓒ Ⓓ

B GRAMMAR IN CONTEXT: Using the Telephone • Weather

Choose the correct answer to complete the conversation.

Example:
_____
- (A) Yes, it is.
- (B) I'm calling.
- ● Hello.
- (D) Goodbye.

12. Hi, Ann. _____
I'm calling from Honolulu.
- (A) Hello.
- (B) Is this Jim?
- (C) Am I Jim?
- (D) This is Jim.

13. _____
How's the weather in Honolulu?
- (A) Hello. This is Ann.
- (B) Hello. Is this Jim?
- (C) Hi, Jim.
- (D) Yes, it is.

14. The weather is beautiful. It's hot and _____.
- (A) snowing
- (B) sunny
- (C) cold
- (D) cool

C INTERPRETING A THERMOMETER

°F	°C	
100	38	(A)
70	21	(B)
50	10	(C)
32	0	(D)

For each weather expression, choose the correct temperature on the thermometer.

Example:
It's warm. (A) ● (C) (D)

15. It's cold.

16. It's hot.

17. It's cool.

D LISTENING ASSESSMENT: Weather Report

Read and listen to the questions. Then listen to the weather report, and answer the questions.

18. How's the weather in Miami?
- (A) It's cool.
- (B) It's raining.
- (C) It's snowing.
- (D) It's sunny.

19. What's the temperature in Los Angeles?
- (A) 40°F.
- (B) 95°F.
- (C) 80°F.
- (D) It's hot.

20. How's the weather in New York?
- (A) It's hot.
- (B) It's cold.
- (C) It's snowing.
- (D) It's warm.

E WRITING ASSESSMENT: Form

Name: _____

Social Security Number: _____

Marital Status: _____

F SPEAKING ASSESSMENT

I can ask and answer these questions:

Ask Answer
- ☐ ☐ What's your marital status?
- ☐ ☐ Are you married or single?
- ☐ ☐ How's the weather today?

12 (A) (B) (C) (D)   15 (A) (B) (C) (D)   18 (A) (B) (C) (D)
13 (A) (B) (C) (D)   16 (A) (B) (C) (D)   19 (A) (B) (C) (D)
14 (A) (B) (C) (D)   17 (A) (B) (C) (D)   20 (A) (B) (C) (D)

B 14

STOP

Name _____

Date _____ Class _____

6

A FAMILY RELATIONS

Look at the picture. Choose the correct answer.

John   Kate

Billy   Ann

Example:

John is Kate's _____.
- Ⓐ wife
- Ⓑ husband
- Ⓒ daughter
- Ⓓ son   Ⓐ ● Ⓒ Ⓓ

1. Billy is John and Kate's _____.
- Ⓐ brother
- Ⓑ father
- Ⓒ uncle
- Ⓓ son

2. Ann is Billy's _____.
- Ⓐ daughter
- Ⓑ cousin
- Ⓒ sister
- Ⓓ mother

3. John and Kate are Billy and Ann's _____.
- Ⓐ children
- Ⓑ parents
- Ⓒ grandparents
- Ⓓ aunt and uncle

Look at the picture. Choose the correct answer.

Henry   Peggy

Kate

Billy   Ann

4. Henry is Billy and Ann's _____.
- Ⓐ grandson
- Ⓑ granddaughter
- Ⓒ grandfather
- Ⓓ grandmother

5. Ann is Peggy and Henry's _____.
- Ⓐ granddaughter
- Ⓑ daughter
- Ⓒ mother
- Ⓓ sister

6. Henry and Peggy are Billy and Ann's _____.
- Ⓐ children
- Ⓑ parents
- Ⓒ grandparents
- Ⓓ grandchildren

7. Ann and Billy are Henry and Peggy's _____.
- Ⓐ children
- Ⓑ grandparents
- Ⓒ parents
- Ⓓ grandchildren

. . . .

1 Ⓐ Ⓑ Ⓒ Ⓓ   3 Ⓐ Ⓑ Ⓒ Ⓓ   5 Ⓐ Ⓑ Ⓒ Ⓓ   7 Ⓐ Ⓑ Ⓒ Ⓓ

2 Ⓐ Ⓑ Ⓒ Ⓓ   4 Ⓐ Ⓑ Ⓒ Ⓓ   6 Ⓐ Ⓑ Ⓒ Ⓓ

 Go to the next page

Choose the correct answer.

Example:

My_____ is feeding his cat.
- (A) daughter
- (B) wife
- (C) uncle
- (D) mother

(A) (B) ● (D)

11. My _____ is painting her living room.
- (A) aunt
- (B) uncle
- (C) father
- (D) brother

8. My _____ is doing her homework.
- (A) brother
- (B) son
- (C) nephew
- (D) niece

12. My _____ are doing their exercises.
- (A) sisters
- (B) parents
- (C) aunts
- (D) nieces

9. My _____ is washing his hair.
- (A) niece
- (B) nephew
- (C) aunt
- (D) cousins

13. _____ her windows.
- (A) My brother is watching
- (B) My sister is watching
- (C) My brother is washing
- (D) My sister is washing

10. My _____ are brushing their teeth.
- (A) aunt
- (B) uncle
- (C) cousins
- (D) sister

14. _____ TV.
- (A) My parents are washing
- (B) My uncles are washing
- (C) My aunt and uncle are watching
- (D) My aunts are watching

....

8 (A) (B) (C) (D)   10 (A) (B) (C) (D)   12 (A) (B) (C) (D)   14 (A) (B) (C) (D)

9 (A) (B) (C) (D)   11 (A) (B) (C) (D)   13 (A) (B) (C) (D)

Go to the next page ⇒

C GRAMMAR IN CONTEXT: Greeting & Introducing

Choose the correct answer to complete the conversation.

Example:

Hello. _____
- Ⓐ Is this Brenda?
- Ⓑ How are you?
- Ⓒ Who are you?
- Ⓓ How's the weather?

16. Fine, thanks.
_____ my sister.
- Ⓐ I'm
- Ⓑ Nice to meet
- Ⓒ Her name is
- Ⓓ I'd like to introduce

15. Fine. _____
- Ⓐ Where are you?
- Ⓑ What are you doing?
- Ⓒ And you?
- Ⓓ Yes, I am.

17. _____
- Ⓐ Fine, thanks.
- Ⓑ And you?
- Ⓒ Nice to meet you.
- Ⓓ Nice to meet you, too.

D LISTENING ASSESSMENT

Read and listen to the questions. Then listen to the story, and answer the questions.

18. What day is it?
- Ⓐ It's a beautiful day.
- Ⓑ He's happy.
- Ⓒ It's his wedding day.
- Ⓓ It's his birthday.

19. What are his parents doing?
- Ⓐ They're eating cake.
- Ⓑ They're sitting in the living room.
- Ⓒ They're dancing.
- Ⓓ They're taking photographs.

20. What's his grandfather doing?
- Ⓐ He's dancing.
- Ⓑ He's taking photographs.
- Ⓒ He's eating cake.
- Ⓓ He's old.

E LEARNING SKILL: Categorizing

Write each word in the correct column.

| aunt | daughter | husband | sister | uncle |
| brother | father | mother | son | wife |

Male   **Female**

_____brother_____   _____aunt_____

_____   _____

_____   _____

_____   _____

F EYE CONTACT & GESTURES

For each sentence, choose the correct picture.

A

B

C

D

1. "Patty, this is Mr. Fisher."   _____

2. "I'd like to introduce my sister."   _____

3. "May I ask a question?"   _____

4. "Hello. My name is Peter."   _____

G WRITING ASSESSMENT

Write about the people in your family—sisters, brothers, parents, children, grandparents.
What are their names? (Use a separate sheet of paper.)

H SPEAKING ASSESSMENT

I can introduce myself and others:

Say Respond

☐ ☐ I'm _____.
☐ ☐ I'd like to introduce
       _____.

I can ask and answer these questions:

Ask Answer

☐ ☐ Who is in your family?
       Who are the people in
         your family?
☐ ☐ What are their names?

I can talk about a photograph:

Ask Answer

☐ ☐ Who is he/she?
       Who are they?
☐ ☐ What's his/her name?
       What are their names?
☐ ☐ What's he/she doing?
       What are they doing?

STOP

A IDENTIFYING & LOCATING PLACES IN THE COMMUNITY

Choose the correct answer.

1. The _____ is next to the park.
   - Ⓐ clinic
   - Ⓑ hotel
   - Ⓒ school
   - Ⓓ supermarket

2. The laundromat is _____ the bakery and the bookstore.
   - Ⓐ across from
   - Ⓑ around the corner from
   - Ⓒ next
   - Ⓓ between

3. The _____ is around the corner from the hospital.
   - Ⓐ restaurant
   - Ⓑ department store
   - Ⓒ cafeteria
   - Ⓓ supermarket

4. The library is _____ the gas station.
   - Ⓐ across from
   - Ⓑ around the corner from
   - Ⓒ next
   - Ⓓ between

B IDENTIFYING ROOMS, FURNITURE, & FIXTURES IN A RESIDENCE

5. There's a new _____ in the _____.
   - Ⓐ closet . . bedroom
   - Ⓑ refrigerator . . bathroom
   - Ⓒ stove . . kitchen
   - Ⓓ refrigerator . . kitchen

6. Is there a _____ in the _____?
   - Ⓐ window . . bathroom
   - Ⓑ closet . . bedroom
   - Ⓒ closet . . living room
   - Ⓓ basement . . bedroom

7. There's a very nice _____ in the _____.
   - Ⓐ sofa . . living room
   - Ⓑ bed . . bedroom
   - Ⓒ window . . living room
   - Ⓓ TV . . living room

8. How many _____ are there in the _____?
   - Ⓐ closets . . floor
   - Ⓑ floors . . apartment
   - Ⓒ elevators . . building
   - Ⓓ apartments . . building

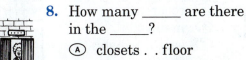

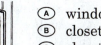

1 Ⓐ Ⓑ Ⓒ Ⓓ   4 Ⓐ Ⓑ Ⓒ Ⓓ   7 Ⓐ Ⓑ Ⓒ Ⓓ

2 Ⓐ Ⓑ Ⓒ Ⓓ   5 Ⓐ Ⓑ Ⓒ Ⓓ   8 Ⓐ Ⓑ Ⓒ Ⓓ

3 Ⓐ Ⓑ Ⓒ Ⓓ   6 Ⓐ Ⓑ Ⓒ Ⓓ

Go to the next page

C GRAMMAR IN CONTEXT: Inquiring About Residences, Rentals, & Neighborhoods

Choose the correct answer to complete each conversation.

Example:
Excuse me. _____ a bank in this neighborhood?
- Ⓐ There
- Ⓑ Where
- Ⓒ Are there
- ● Is there

9. Yes. _____ a bank on State Street.
- Ⓐ There
- Ⓑ There's
- Ⓒ There are
- Ⓓ It's

10. _____
- Ⓐ Thank.
- Ⓑ Thanks you.
- Ⓒ Thank you.
- Ⓓ Yes.

11. _____
- Ⓐ Welcome.
- Ⓑ Yes, there is.
- Ⓒ Thanks.
- Ⓓ You're welcome.

12. How many bedrooms _____ in the house?
- Ⓐ is there
- Ⓑ are there
- Ⓒ there is
- Ⓓ there are

13. _____ three bedrooms.
- Ⓐ There
- Ⓑ There's
- Ⓒ They are
- Ⓓ There are

14. _____ condominiums _____ in the complex?
- Ⓐ How . . are there
- Ⓑ How . . there are
- Ⓒ How many . . are there
- Ⓓ How many . . there are

15. _____ fifty condos.
- Ⓐ Are
- Ⓑ There
- Ⓒ There are
- Ⓓ Are there

16. Is there a _____ in the apartment building?
- Ⓐ cockroach
- Ⓑ mailbox
- Ⓒ satellite dish
- Ⓓ superintendent

17. Yes. His apartment is in the _____.
- Ⓐ basement
- Ⓑ window
- Ⓒ wall
- Ⓓ roof

Name _____ Date _____

LISTENING ASSESSMENT

Read and listen to the questions. Then listen to the conversation, and answer the questions.

18. How many bedrooms are there in the apartment?
- Ⓐ Six.
- Ⓑ Three.
- Ⓒ One.
- Ⓓ Two.

19. How many bathrooms are there?
- Ⓐ Six.
- Ⓑ Three.
- Ⓒ One.
- Ⓓ Two.

20. Where's the laundromat?
- Ⓐ It's next to the building.
- Ⓑ It's next to the supermarket.
- Ⓒ It's across from the building.
- Ⓓ It's across from the post office.

E **SPEAKING ASSESSMENT: Information Gap (Part A)**

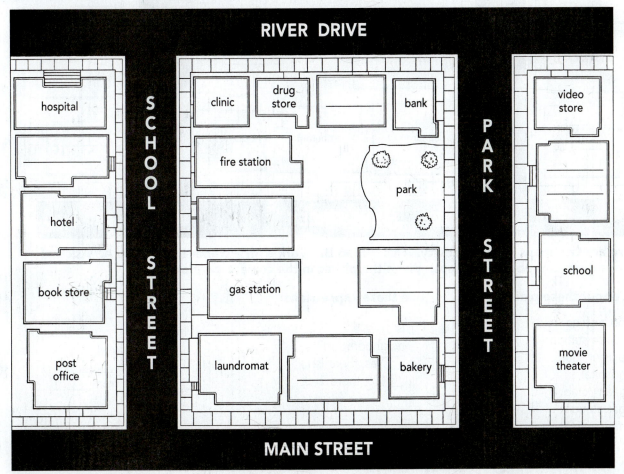

There are two maps for this activity. This is Map A. Work with a student with Map B. Ask and answer questions about the maps. Write the places in the correct locations.

Ask about these places:
- ☐ bus station
- ☐ library
- ☐ cafeteria
- ☐ department store
- ☐ supermarket
- ☐ hair salon
- ☐ restaurant

Use these expressions:
- ☐ Is there a _____ in this neighborhood?
  - ☐ Yes, there is.
  - ☐ No, there isn't.

- ☐ Where's the _____?
- ☐ It's on _street_.
- ☐ It's next to _____.
- ☐ It's across from _____.
- ☐ It's between _____.
- ☐ It's around the corner from _____.

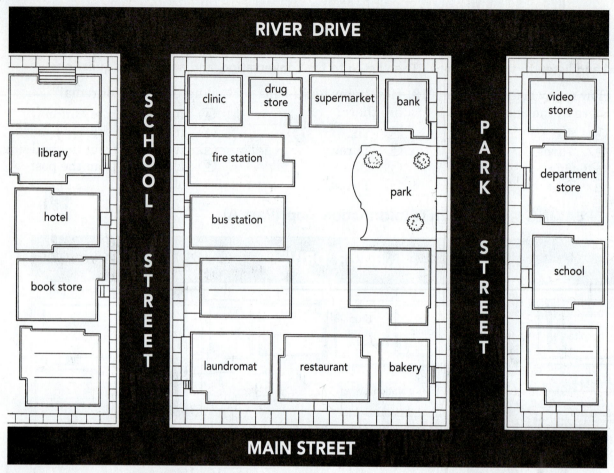

There are two maps for this activity. This is Map B. Work with a student with Map A. Ask and answer questions about the maps. Write the places in the correct locations.

Ask about these places:

- [ ] post office
- [ ] police station
- [ ] barber shop
- [ ] hospital
- [ ] health club
- [ ] gas station
- [ ] movie theater

Use these expressions:

- [ ] Is there a _____ in this neighborhood?
  - [ ] Yes, there is.
  - [ ] No, there isn't.

- [ ] Where's the _____?
  - [ ] It's on _street_ .
  - [ ] It's next to _____.
  - [ ] It's across from _____.
  - [ ] It's between _____.
  - [ ] It's around the corner from _____.

F WRITING ASSESSMENT

Write a paragraph about your neighborhood.

....

....

....

....

STOP

A CLOTHING

Choose the correct answer.

Example:

I'm looking for _____.
- Ⓐ pants
- Ⓑ a blouse
- ● a dress
- Ⓓ a suit

6. Excuse me. I think that's my _____.
- Ⓐ boots
- Ⓑ coat
- Ⓒ gloves
- Ⓓ shoes

1. I'm looking for _____.
- Ⓐ a sock
- Ⓑ a suit
- Ⓒ a skirt
- Ⓓ a shirt

7. _____ are over there.
- Ⓐ Sweater
- Ⓑ Sweaters
- Ⓒ A sock
- Ⓓ A pair of socks

2. I need _____.
- Ⓐ a shoe
- Ⓑ a pair of shoe
- Ⓒ a pair of shoes
- Ⓓ pairs of shoe

8. _____ your glasses?
- Ⓐ Is this
- Ⓑ Is that
- Ⓒ Are these
- Ⓓ Are you sure

3. Here's a nice _____.
- Ⓐ tie
- Ⓑ belt
- Ⓒ watch
- Ⓓ necklace

9. _____ very nice hat!
- Ⓐ This
- Ⓑ That's
- Ⓒ These are
- Ⓓ That's a

4. _____ your watch?
- Ⓐ Are these
- Ⓑ Are those
- Ⓒ Is this
- Ⓓ I think

10. Is this your jacket?
- Ⓐ Yes, they are.
- Ⓑ No, they aren't.
- Ⓒ No, I'm not.
- Ⓓ No, it isn't.

5. _____ jeans are blue.
- Ⓐ Those
- Ⓑ That
- Ⓒ This
- Ⓓ Here's

11. Excuse me. I'm looking for a gray suit.
- Ⓐ Gray shirts are very popular.
- Ⓑ I'm sorry. All our suits are gray.
- Ⓒ Suits are over there.
- Ⓓ I think this is my suit.

1 Ⓐ Ⓑ Ⓒ Ⓓ   4 Ⓐ Ⓑ Ⓒ Ⓓ   7 Ⓐ Ⓑ Ⓒ Ⓓ   10 Ⓐ Ⓑ Ⓒ Ⓓ

2 Ⓐ Ⓑ Ⓒ Ⓓ   5 Ⓐ Ⓑ Ⓒ Ⓓ   8 Ⓐ Ⓑ Ⓒ Ⓓ   11 Ⓐ Ⓑ Ⓒ Ⓓ

3 Ⓐ Ⓑ Ⓒ Ⓓ   6 Ⓐ Ⓑ Ⓒ Ⓓ   9 Ⓐ Ⓑ Ⓒ Ⓓ

Go to the next page   **23**

GRAMMAR IN CONTEXT: Asking for Help • Identifying Clothing Needs

Choose the correct answer to complete the conversation.

Example:

May I help _____?
- Ⓐ me
- Ⓑ my
- ● you
- Ⓓ your

12. Yes, please. I need _____.
- Ⓐ a pair of
- Ⓑ glove
- Ⓒ a pair of glove
- Ⓓ a pair of gloves

13. Excuse me. _____ a brown umbrella.
- Ⓐ I'm looking
- Ⓑ I'm looking for
- Ⓒ You're looking
- Ⓓ You're looking for

14. I'm sorry. All our _____ black.
- Ⓐ umbrella is
- Ⓑ umbrellas is
- Ⓒ umbrella are
- Ⓓ umbrellas are

15. Can you help _____?
- Ⓐ me
- Ⓑ my
- Ⓒ I
- Ⓓ you

Yes.

16. How much _____ coat?
- Ⓐ are these
- Ⓑ are those
- Ⓒ is this
- Ⓓ is it

17. It's very _____. It's 25 dollars.
- Ⓐ clean
- Ⓑ brown
- Ⓒ over there
- Ⓓ inexpensive

C **LISTENING ASSESSMENT**

Read and listen to the questions. Then listen to the conversation, and answer the questions.

18. Where is the conversation taking place?
- Ⓐ In a closet.
- Ⓑ In a laundromat.
- Ⓒ In a store.
- Ⓓ In a restaurant.

19. What's the person looking for?
- Ⓐ Her raincoat.
- Ⓑ Her husband.
- Ⓒ A raincoat for a man.
- Ⓓ A raincoat for a woman.

20. What size is the raincoat?
- Ⓐ He's tall.
- Ⓑ It's large.
- Ⓒ He's short.
- Ⓓ It's small.

. . . .

12 Ⓐ Ⓑ Ⓒ Ⓓ   15 Ⓐ Ⓑ Ⓒ Ⓓ   18 Ⓐ Ⓑ Ⓒ Ⓓ

13 Ⓐ Ⓑ Ⓒ Ⓓ   16 Ⓐ Ⓑ Ⓒ Ⓓ   19 Ⓐ Ⓑ Ⓒ Ⓓ

14 Ⓐ Ⓑ Ⓒ Ⓓ   17 Ⓐ Ⓑ Ⓒ Ⓓ   20 Ⓐ Ⓑ Ⓒ Ⓓ   Go to the next page ⟩

D MONEY: Coins

penny	nickel	dime	quarter	half-dollar
1¢	5¢	10¢	25¢	50¢
$.01	$.05	$.10	$.25	$.50

Choose the correct amount and write it.

3¢	$.05	6¢	$.10	15¢	$.20	35¢	$.50	$.61

1. _____ $ .10 _____   2. _____   3. _____

4. _____   5. _____   6. _____

7. _____   8. _____   9. _____

Write the amount two ways.

10. three nickels   ____15¢____ or ____$.15____

11. two pennies   _____ or _____

12. four dimes   _____ or _____

13. a quarter and a penny   _____ or _____

14. two dimes and a nickel _____ or _____

15. a half-dollar and a dime _____ or _____

Go to the next page

one dollar
$1.00

five dollars
$5.00

ten dollars
$10.00

twenty dollars
$20.00

fifty dollars
$50.00

one hundred dollars
$100.00

Write the correct amount.

1. $ *25.00*

2. _____

3. _____

4. _____

5. _____

6. _____

7.  _____

8.  _____

9.  _____

10. _____

Go to the next page

Name _____   Date _____

F **CLOTHING LABELS: Sizes, Prices, Colors**

Clothing Sizes & Abbreviations

S Small   **M** Medium   **L** Large   **XL** Extra Large

Look at the clothing labels. Answer the questions.

221757-00-1
0001

SMALL

$30.00

1. What size is this?   _____

2. How much is it?   _____

| 30 DEPT. | 27 CLASS | 05 SUB |
277665-700066 SKU
449

SIZE L
OUR PRICE **$8.99**

3. How much is this?   _____

4. What's the size?   _____

107883
H4001
WHITE
— **SIZE** —
36
$18.00
~~$24.00~~

5. This is on sale. What's the price?   _____

6. What size is it?   _____

7. What color is it?   _____

REGULAR FIT

BOYS

100% COTTON
CLR: BLUE

SIZE: M

$21.99

8. How big is this?   _____

9. What's the color?   _____

10. What's the cost?   _____

Go to the next page

Look at the advertisement for clothing. Answer the questions.

1. What's the regular price of the jeans? _____

2. What's the sale price of the jeans? _____

3. How much are the children's sneakers now? _____

4. What are the sizes of the women's blouses? _____

5. What's the regular price of the men's shirts? _____

6. What's the sale price of the men's shirts? _____

7. How much are the women's blouses on sale? _____

H WRITING ASSESSMENT

What are you wearing today? Tell about the clothing and the colors. Write about it on a separate sheet of paper.

I SPEAKING ASSESSMENT

I can ask and answer these questions:

Ask Answer
☐ ☐ What are you wearing today?
☐ ☐ What color is your _clothing item_ ?
☐ ☐ What's your favorite color?

A COMMON ACTIVITIES

Choose the correct answer.

Example:

I _____.
- ● read
- Ⓑ reads
- Ⓒ sing
- Ⓓ sings

1. She _____ Spanish.
- Ⓐ call
- Ⓑ calls
- Ⓒ speak
- Ⓓ speaks

¡Hola!

2. He _____ every day.
- Ⓐ cook
- Ⓑ cooks
- Ⓒ eat
- Ⓓ eats

3. They _____ in an office.
- Ⓐ live
- Ⓑ lives
- Ⓒ work
- Ⓓ works

4. He _____ TV every day.
- Ⓐ watch
- Ⓑ watches
- Ⓒ listen
- Ⓓ listens

5. She _____ to school.
- Ⓐ goes
- Ⓑ visits
- Ⓒ go
- Ⓓ visit

6. Where _____ he live?
- Ⓐ are
- Ⓑ is
- Ⓒ do
- Ⓓ does

7. What languages _____ you speak?
- Ⓐ are
- Ⓑ is
- Ⓒ do
- Ⓓ does

8. What _____ every day?
- Ⓐ do you
- Ⓑ you do
- Ⓒ do
- Ⓓ do you do

9. _____ she work?
- Ⓐ What does
- Ⓑ Where does
- Ⓒ What do
- Ⓓ Where do

10. _____ she do at the office?
- Ⓐ What does
- Ⓑ What do
- Ⓒ Where does
- Ⓓ Where do

11. _____ your parents live?
- Ⓐ What does
- Ⓑ What do
- Ⓒ Where does
- Ⓓ Where do

. . . .

1 Ⓐ Ⓑ Ⓒ Ⓓ   4 Ⓐ Ⓑ Ⓒ Ⓓ   7 Ⓐ Ⓑ Ⓒ Ⓓ   10 Ⓐ Ⓑ Ⓒ Ⓓ

2 Ⓐ Ⓑ Ⓒ Ⓓ   5 Ⓐ Ⓑ Ⓒ Ⓓ   8 Ⓐ Ⓑ Ⓒ Ⓓ   11 Ⓐ Ⓑ Ⓒ Ⓓ

3 Ⓐ Ⓑ Ⓒ Ⓓ   6 Ⓐ Ⓑ Ⓒ Ⓓ   9 Ⓐ Ⓑ Ⓒ Ⓓ

Go to the next page ⟩

B GRAMMAR IN CONTEXT: Social Interactions

Choose the correct answer to complete the conversation.

12. _____ you speak?
- (A) Where do
- (B) Where does
- (C) What language do
- (D) What language does

13. I speak _____.
- (A) Mexico
- (B) Mexican
- (C) Mexico City
- (D) Spanish

14. _____ your son live?
- (A) Where do
- (B) Where does
- (C) What do
- (D) What does

15. _____ in Las Vegas.
- (A) I live
- (B) He lives
- (C) She lives
- (D) They live

16. _____ he do?
- (A) What does
- (B) Where does
- (C) What do
- (D) Where do

17. He _____ in a hotel.
- (A) work
- (B) works
- (C) visit
- (D) visits

C LISTENING ASSESSMENT

Read and listen to the questions. Then listen to the conversation, and answer the questions.

18. Where does she live?
- (A) In Greece.
- (B) In Dallas.
- (C) In a restaurant.
- (D) At work.

19. What does she do at work?
- (A) She watches TV.
- (B) She reads.
- (C) She cooks.
- (D) She plays the piano.

20. What does she do at home?
- (A) She plays the violin.
- (B) She reads the newspaper.
- (C) She watches TV.
- (D) She works.

D WRITING ASSESSMENT: Daily Activities

What do you do at home every day? What do you do at school or at work? Write about your daily activities. (Use a separate sheet of paper.)

E SPEAKING ASSESSMENT

I can ask and answer these questions:

Ask Answer
- ☐ ☐ What's your name?
- ☐ ☐ Where do you live?
- ☐ ☐ What languages do you speak?
- ☐ ☐ What do you do every day?

Ask Answer
- ☐ ☐ What's his/her name?
- ☐ ☐ Where does he/she live?
- ☐ ☐ What languages does he/she speak?
- ☐ ☐ What does he/she do everyday?

· ·

12 (A) (B) (C) (D)   14 (A) (B) (C) (D)   16 (A) (B) (C) (D)   18 (A) (B) (C) (D)
13 (A) (B) (C) (D)   15 (A) (B) (C) (D)   17 (A) (B) (C) (D)   19 (A) (B) (C) (D)
                                                                  20 (A) (B) (C) (D)

STOP

A COMMON ACTIVITIES: Daily Life, Sports, & Recreation

Choose the best answer.

Example:

Tom _____ basketball on Saturday. He plays basketball on Friday.

- Ⓐ play
- Ⓑ doesn't play
- Ⓒ don't play
- Ⓓ not play   Ⓐ ● Ⓒ Ⓓ

1. My wife and I _____ on Sunday. We go to a restaurant.
   - Ⓐ don't cook
   - Ⓑ doesn't cook
   - Ⓒ don't we cook
   - Ⓓ not cook

2. _____ Janet play tennis on Monday?
   - Ⓐ Is
   - Ⓑ Do
   - Ⓒ Don't
   - Ⓓ Does

3. _____ your parents watch TV?
   - Ⓐ Does
   - Ⓑ Are
   - Ⓒ Do
   - Ⓓ What

4. Does Mr. Lee ride his bike to work?
   - Ⓐ Yes, they do.
   - Ⓑ Yes, it does.
   - Ⓒ Yes, I do.
   - Ⓓ Yes, he does.

5. Do you and your friends play baseball?
   - Ⓐ Yes, we do.
   - Ⓑ Yes, they do.
   - Ⓒ Yes, he does.
   - Ⓓ Yes, it does.

6. Do you play a musical instrument?
   - Ⓐ Yes, they do.
   - Ⓑ Yes, you do.
   - Ⓒ No, I don't.
   - Ⓓ No, it doesn't.

7. What do your friends do on the weekend?
   - Ⓐ Yes, we do.
   - Ⓑ Yes, they do.
   - Ⓒ They play football.
   - Ⓓ I play football.

8. _____ movies do you like?
   - Ⓐ What kind
   - Ⓑ What kind of
   - Ⓒ What's your favorite
   - Ⓓ Who's your favorite

9. My parents _____ go to concerts because my father _____ like classical music.
   - Ⓐ don't . . don't
   - Ⓑ doesn't . . doesn't
   - Ⓒ doesn't . . don't
   - Ⓓ don't . . doesn't

10. My brother _____ very popular. He _____ to a lot of parties.
    - Ⓐ is . . go
    - Ⓑ does . . go
    - Ⓒ is . . goes
    - Ⓓ does . . goes

11. I _____ comedies, and my sister _____ dramas.
    - Ⓐ like . . like
    - Ⓑ like . . likes
    - Ⓒ likes . . likes
    - Ⓓ likes . . like

• •

1 Ⓐ Ⓑ Ⓒ Ⓓ   4 Ⓐ Ⓑ Ⓒ Ⓓ   7 Ⓐ Ⓑ Ⓒ Ⓓ   10 Ⓐ Ⓑ Ⓒ Ⓓ

2 Ⓐ Ⓑ Ⓒ Ⓓ   5 Ⓐ Ⓑ Ⓒ Ⓓ   8 Ⓐ Ⓑ Ⓒ Ⓓ   11 Ⓐ Ⓑ Ⓒ Ⓓ

3 Ⓐ Ⓑ Ⓒ Ⓓ   6 Ⓐ Ⓑ Ⓒ Ⓓ   9 Ⓐ Ⓑ Ⓒ Ⓓ

Go to the next page ⟩

B GRAMMAR IN CONTEXT: Ordering in a Fast Food Restaurant

Read the story. Then choose the correct answer to complete each conversation.

Fran's Fast Food Restaurant is a very special place. Every day Fran cooks a different kind of fast food. On Monday she cooks hamburgers. On Tuesday she cooks cheeseburgers. On Wednesday she makes tacos. On Thursday she makes pizza. On Friday she cooks chicken. On Saturday she cooks hot dogs. And on Sunday she makes sandwiches.

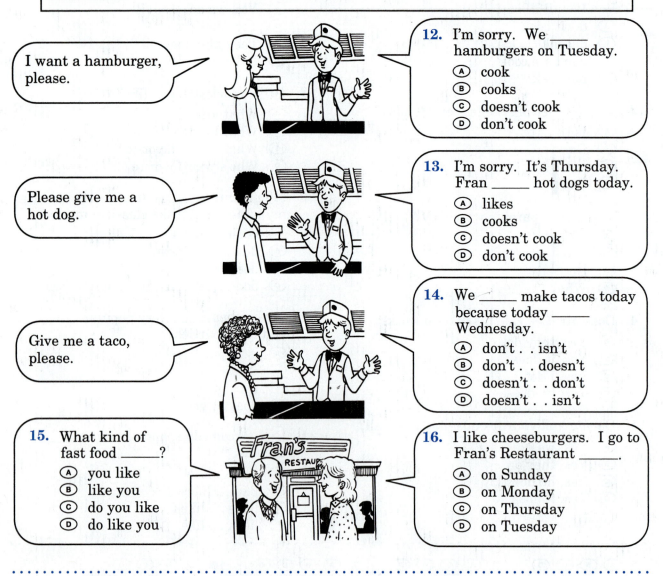

12. I'm sorry. We _____ hamburgers on Tuesday.
- Ⓐ cook
- Ⓑ cooks
- Ⓒ doesn't cook
- Ⓓ don't cook

13. I'm sorry. It's Thursday. Fran _____ hot dogs today.
- Ⓐ likes
- Ⓑ cooks
- Ⓒ doesn't cook
- Ⓓ don't cook

14. We _____ make tacos today because today _____ Wednesday.
- Ⓐ don't . . isn't
- Ⓑ don't . . doesn't
- Ⓒ doesn't . . don't
- Ⓓ doesn't . . isn't

15. What kind of fast food _____?
- Ⓐ you like
- Ⓑ like you
- Ⓒ do you like
- Ⓓ do like you

16. I like cheeseburgers. I go to Fran's Restaurant _____.
- Ⓐ on Sunday
- Ⓑ on Monday
- Ⓒ on Thursday
- Ⓓ on Tuesday

- -

12 Ⓐ Ⓑ Ⓒ Ⓓ   14 Ⓐ Ⓑ Ⓒ Ⓓ   16 Ⓐ Ⓑ Ⓒ Ⓓ

13 Ⓐ Ⓑ Ⓒ Ⓓ   15 Ⓐ Ⓑ Ⓒ Ⓓ

Go to the next page ⟩

Name _____   Date _____

C LISTENING ASSESSMENT

Read and listen to the questions. Then listen to the story, and answer the questions.

17. What do they do on Tuesday?
    - Ⓐ They jog.
    - Ⓑ They play tennis.
    - Ⓒ They play golf.
    - Ⓓ They play basketball.

18. Do they ride their bikes on Wednesday?
    - Ⓐ Yes, he does.
    - Ⓑ Yes, she does.
    - Ⓒ Yes, they do.
    - Ⓓ No, they don't.

19. What do they do on Friday?
    - Ⓐ They play golf.
    - Ⓑ They play basketball.
    - Ⓒ He plays golf, and she plays basketball.
    - Ⓓ She plays golf, and he plays basketball.

20. What do they do on the weekend?
    - Ⓐ She does yoga, and he swims.
    - Ⓑ They jog.
    - Ⓒ They go to a health club.
    - Ⓓ They're very athletic people.

D WRITING & GRAMMAR ASSESSMENT

Write the correct words to complete the sentences.

1. I ___live___ in New York.   He ___lives___ in Los Angeles.

2. I _____ in a bank.   She _____ in an office.

3. I _____ a taxi.   He _____ a bus.

4. I _____ the piano.   She _____ the violin.

5. I _____ the newspaper.   He _____ books.

6. I _____ to movies.   She _____ to concerts.

7. I _____ English.   He _____ Spanish.

8. I _____ TV.   She _____ videos.

17 Ⓐ Ⓑ Ⓒ Ⓓ   19 Ⓐ Ⓑ Ⓒ Ⓓ
18 Ⓐ Ⓑ Ⓒ Ⓓ   20 Ⓐ Ⓑ Ⓒ Ⓓ

Go to the next page ⟹   **33**

E WRITING ASSESSMENT: Days of the Week

Look at the abbreviation. Write the correct day of the week.

MON _____Monday_____   THU _____

FRI _____   SUN _____

TUE _____   WED _____

SAT _____

F WRITING ASSESSMENT: Recreation & Entertainment Activities

What do you do on the weekend? How do you spend your time? Write a paragraph about it.

....

....

....

....

....

G SPEAKING ASSESSMENT

I can ask and answer these questions:

Ask Answer

☐ ☐ What do you do during the week?
☐ ☐ What do you do on the weekend?

☐ ☐ Do you like *Italian/ Greek / Chinese / Puerto Rican / Japanese / Mexican / American* food?
☐ ☐ What kind of food do you like?

☐ ☐ Do you like *comedies / dramas / westerns / adventure movies / science fiction movies / cartoons*?
☐ ☐ What kind of movies do you like?

☐ ☐ Do you like *novels / poetry / short stories / non-fiction / biographies*?
☐ ☐ What kind of books do you like?

☐ ☐ Do you like *comedies / dramas / cartoons / game shows / news programs*?
☐ ☐ What kind of TV programs do you like?

☐ ☐ Do you like *classical music / popular music / jazz / rock music / country music*?
☐ ☐ What kind of music do you like?

☐ ☐ Do you like *football / baseball / soccer / golf / hockey / tennis*?
☐ ☐ What kind of sports do you like?

STOP

A FAMILY RELATIONS

Choose the correct answer.

1. My grandparents live in Chicago. We call _____ every Sunday.
   - Ⓐ him
   - Ⓑ her
   - Ⓒ us
   - Ⓓ them

2. My uncle is in the hospital. My aunt visits _____ there every day.
   - Ⓐ him
   - Ⓑ her
   - Ⓒ me
   - Ⓓ them

3. Our son's wife is very nice. We like _____ very much.
   - Ⓐ it
   - Ⓑ him
   - Ⓒ her
   - Ⓓ them

4. My father usually washes his car on Thursday. He rarely washes _____ on Friday.
   - Ⓐ her
   - Ⓑ him
   - Ⓒ it
   - Ⓓ them

5. We talk to our daughter every weekend. She always calls _____ on Saturday.
   - Ⓐ him
   - Ⓑ us
   - Ⓒ we
   - Ⓓ her

6. You're my very close friend. I think about _____ all the time.
   - Ⓐ me
   - Ⓑ your
   - Ⓒ you
   - Ⓓ them

7. My sister always studies in the library. She _____ studies in her room.
   - Ⓐ always
   - Ⓑ usually
   - Ⓒ sometimes
   - Ⓓ never

8. My parents _____ a small apartment.
   - Ⓐ has
   - Ⓑ live
   - Ⓒ in
   - Ⓓ have

9. Their son _____ brown hair.
   - Ⓐ has
   - Ⓑ have
   - Ⓒ is
   - Ⓓ his

10. Our neighbors _____ a new satellite dish.
   - Ⓐ are
   - Ⓑ never
   - Ⓒ has
   - Ⓓ have

11. I _____ one sister. My sister _____ blue eyes.
   - Ⓐ have . . have
   - Ⓑ has . . have
   - Ⓒ have . . has
   - Ⓓ have . . is

12. My brother _____ curly hair. My sisters _____ straight hair.
   - Ⓐ have . . have
   - Ⓑ has . . have
   - Ⓒ have . . has
   - Ⓓ has . . has

1 Ⓐ Ⓑ Ⓒ Ⓓ 4 Ⓐ Ⓑ Ⓒ Ⓓ 7 Ⓐ Ⓑ Ⓒ Ⓓ 10 Ⓐ Ⓑ Ⓒ Ⓓ
2 Ⓐ Ⓑ Ⓒ Ⓓ 5 Ⓐ Ⓑ Ⓒ Ⓓ 8 Ⓐ Ⓑ Ⓒ Ⓓ 11 Ⓐ Ⓑ Ⓒ Ⓓ
3 Ⓐ Ⓑ Ⓒ Ⓓ 6 Ⓐ Ⓑ Ⓒ Ⓓ 9 Ⓐ Ⓑ Ⓒ Ⓓ 12 Ⓐ Ⓑ Ⓒ Ⓓ

Go to the next page

GRAMMAR IN CONTEXT: Asking for Tableware • Describing Oneself

Choose the correct answer to complete the conversation.

Excuse me. I need a fork and knife, please.

13. Here you are. _____ eat pizza with a fork and knife?
- Ⓐ You usually
- Ⓑ You do usually
- Ⓒ Do you usually
- Ⓓ Do usually

14. Yes. _____ a spoon for my granddaughter?
- Ⓐ You have
- Ⓑ Do you have
- Ⓒ You do have
- Ⓓ Do have

15. Yes. _____ eat spaghetti with a spoon?
- Ⓐ Always
- Ⓑ She always
- Ⓒ Is she always
- Ⓓ Does she always

Yes. Always.

16. _____ look like?
- Ⓐ Who you
- Ⓑ Who do you
- Ⓒ Do you
- Ⓓ How often do you

17. I look like my brother. We both have _____ hair.
- Ⓐ tall
- Ⓑ heavy
- Ⓒ brown
- Ⓓ different

C **LISTENING ASSESSMENT**

Read and listen to the questions. Then listen to the story, and answer the questions.

18. How does this person look like her sister?
- Ⓐ They're both short.
- Ⓑ They both have brown eyes.
- Ⓒ They both have long hair.
- Ⓓ They both have brown hair.

19. Where does the teacher live?
- Ⓐ In the suburbs.
- Ⓑ In the city.
- Ⓒ In a small apartment.
- Ⓓ In a school.

20. What do they do every day?
- Ⓐ They watch videos.
- Ⓑ They talk on the telephone.
- Ⓒ They go to parties.
- Ⓓ They're very different.

D **WRITING ASSESSMENT**

Write about yourself and another person. Do you look like this person? Describe how you and this person are different. (Use a separate sheet of paper.)

E **SPEAKING ASSESSMENT**

I can ask and answer these questions:

Ask Answer
- ☐ ☐ Do you have any brothers or sisters?
- ☐ ☐ Tell me about your family. (I have . . .)

- ☐ ☐ Tell me about a family member or a friend:
- ☐ ☐ What's his/her name?
- ☐ ☐ What does he/she look like?
- ☐ ☐ What does he/she do?

A DESCRIBING STATES OF BEING

1. Is he happy?
- Ⓐ No. He's tired.
- Ⓑ No. He's angry.
- Ⓒ No. He's sad.
- Ⓓ No. He's nervous.

5. Why are you perspiring?
- Ⓐ I'm cold.
- Ⓑ I'm happy.
- Ⓒ I'm hot.
- Ⓓ I'm angry.

2. Is she hungry?
- Ⓐ No. She's happy.
- Ⓑ No. She's thirsty.
- Ⓒ No. She's cold.
- Ⓓ No. She's scared.

6. What do you do when you're tired?
- Ⓐ I yawn.
- Ⓑ I'm yawning.
- Ⓒ We're smiling.
- Ⓓ You shout.

3. Is he tired?
- Ⓐ No. He's scared.
- Ⓑ No. He's sick.
- Ⓒ No. He's hungry.
- Ⓓ No. He's angry.

7. _____ when I'm nervous.
- Ⓐ I'm blushing
- Ⓑ I'm perspiring
- Ⓒ I'm biting my nails
- Ⓓ I always bite my nails

4. Are they cold?
- Ⓐ Yes. They cry.
- Ⓑ Yes. They're crying.
- Ⓒ Yes. They shiver.
- Ⓓ Yes. They're shivering.

8. _____ because she's happy today.
- Ⓐ She smiles
- Ⓑ She's smiling
- Ⓒ She always smiles
- Ⓓ She never smiles

B GRAMMAR IN CONTEXT: Asking About Home Activities

9. _____ doing?
- Ⓐ What do you
- Ⓑ What are you
- Ⓒ Why do you
- Ⓓ Why are you

10. _____ the rug with a broom.
- Ⓐ I sweep
- Ⓑ I walk
- Ⓒ I'm sweeping
- Ⓓ I'm walking

11. _____ the rug with a broom?
- Ⓐ Are you usually walking
- Ⓑ Are you usually sleeping
- Ⓒ Do you usually walk
- Ⓓ Do you usually sweep

12. No. My _____ is broken.
- Ⓐ vacuum
- Ⓑ flashlight
- Ⓒ hammer
- Ⓓ computer

1 Ⓐ Ⓑ Ⓒ Ⓓ   4 Ⓐ Ⓑ Ⓒ Ⓓ   7 Ⓐ Ⓑ Ⓒ Ⓓ   10 Ⓐ Ⓑ Ⓒ Ⓓ

2 Ⓐ Ⓑ Ⓒ Ⓓ   5 Ⓐ Ⓑ Ⓒ Ⓓ   8 Ⓐ Ⓑ Ⓒ Ⓓ   11 Ⓐ Ⓑ Ⓒ Ⓓ

3 Ⓐ Ⓑ Ⓒ Ⓓ   6 Ⓐ Ⓑ Ⓒ Ⓓ   9 Ⓐ Ⓑ Ⓒ Ⓓ   12 Ⓐ Ⓑ Ⓒ Ⓓ

Go to the next page

C READING

Read the story. Then answer the questions.

> It isn't a typical Monday morning at the Lane family's apartment. Mr. Lane usually takes the train to his laboratory, but he isn't taking the train today. Mrs. Lane usually drives to her office, but she isn't driving there today. Jimmy and Jennifer Lane usually take the bus to school, but they aren't taking the bus today. And Julie Lane usually rides her bicycle to her job at the shopping mall, but she isn't riding her bicycle there today. It's snowing very hard this morning. The streets are empty, and the city is quiet. Everybody in town is staying home.

13. Who usually goes to work in a car?

   Ⓐ Mr. Lane.
   Ⓑ Mrs. Lane.
   Ⓒ Jimmy Lane.
   Ⓓ Julie Lane.

14. How do the young children in the family usually go to school?

   Ⓐ They take the train.
   Ⓑ They're taking the train.
   Ⓒ They take the bus.
   Ⓓ They're taking the bus.

15. Who works in a store?

   Ⓐ Mr. Lane.
   Ⓑ Mrs. Lane.
   Ⓒ Jennifer Lane.
   Ⓓ Julie Lane.

16. Why is everybody in town staying home this morning?

   Ⓐ The streets are empty.
   Ⓑ The city is quiet.
   Ⓒ It's snowing.
   Ⓓ It's cold.

D LISTENING ASSESSMENT

Read and listen to the questions. Then listen to the conversation, and answer the questions.

17. What does Wanda do at the office?

   Ⓐ She answers the telephone.
   Ⓑ She sorts the mail.
   Ⓒ She cleans the office.
   Ⓓ She types all the letters.

18. Who cleans the office?

   Ⓐ Ken.
   Ⓑ Mrs. Kent.
   Ⓒ George.
   Ⓓ Nancy.

19. What's Nancy's job?

   Ⓐ She's sick today.
   Ⓑ She's at home with the flu.
   Ⓒ She usually types letters.
   Ⓓ She's typing letters today.

20. Where's Mrs. Kent?

   Ⓐ She's with the president.
   Ⓑ She's at home with the flu.
   Ⓒ She's the boss.
   Ⓓ She's at the dentist.

E WRITING ASSESSMENT: States of Being

What do you usually do when you're happy? sad? tired? hungry? thirsty? Write about it on a separate sheet of paper.

F SPEAKING ASSESSMENT

I can ask and answer these questions:

Ask Answer
☐ ☐ Are you hungry?
☐ ☐ Are you thirsty?
☐ ☐ Are you *happy/sad/tired*?
☐ ☐ Why are you *happy/sad/tired*?

Ask Answer
☐ ☐ How do you go to school?
☐ ☐ Do you drive a car?
☐ ☐ Do you take a bus/train?
☐ ☐ Do you walk?
☐ ☐ Do you ride a bicycle?

- -

13 Ⓐ Ⓑ Ⓒ Ⓓ   15 Ⓐ Ⓑ Ⓒ Ⓓ   17 Ⓐ Ⓑ Ⓒ Ⓓ   19 Ⓐ Ⓑ Ⓒ Ⓓ

14 Ⓐ Ⓑ Ⓒ Ⓓ   16 Ⓐ Ⓑ Ⓒ Ⓓ   18 Ⓐ Ⓑ Ⓒ Ⓓ   20 Ⓐ Ⓑ Ⓒ Ⓓ

A OCCUPATIONS, ABILITIES, & SKILLS

1. What's his job?
- Ⓐ He's a teacher.
- Ⓑ He's a singer.
- Ⓒ He's a baker.
- Ⓓ He's an actor.

2. What's her occupation?
- Ⓐ She's a dancer.
- Ⓑ She's a chef.
- Ⓒ She's a secretary.
- Ⓓ She's a mechanic.

3. Can he type?
Yes. He's _____.
- Ⓐ a superintendent
- Ⓑ a secretary
- Ⓒ a salesperson
- Ⓓ a computer

4. What can you do?
I can _____.
- Ⓐ use a cash register
- Ⓑ use a calculator
- Ⓒ use business software
- Ⓓ use a computer

5. I can cook.
- Ⓐ I'm a construction worker.
- Ⓑ I'm a chef.
- Ⓒ I'm a mechanic.
- Ⓓ I'm a driver.

6. She can talk to customers.
- Ⓐ She's a teacher.
- Ⓑ She's a singer.
- Ⓒ She's a salesperson.
- Ⓓ She's a dancer.

7. He can build things.
- Ⓐ He's a mechanic.
- Ⓑ He's a salesperson.
- Ⓒ He's a building superintendent.
- Ⓓ He's a construction worker.

8. Tell me about your skills.
- Ⓐ I'm looking for work.
- Ⓑ I'm looking for a job as a secretary.
- Ⓒ I can file and type.
- Ⓓ I'm a salesperson.

B GRAMMAR IN CONTEXT: Requesting Permission to Leave Work • Calling to Explain Absence

9. May I leave work early today?
_____ go to the doctor.
- Ⓐ You have
- Ⓑ You have to
- Ⓒ I have
- Ⓓ I have to

10. Okay. _____ leave early.
- Ⓐ You have to
- Ⓑ You can
- Ⓒ I have to
- Ⓓ I can

11. I'm sorry. _____ come to work today. I'm sick.
- Ⓐ You can
- Ⓑ I can
- Ⓒ I can't
- Ⓓ I have to

12. That's okay. _____ come to work.
- Ⓐ Don't have to
- Ⓑ You don't have to
- Ⓒ I have to
- Ⓓ I don't have to

1 Ⓐ Ⓑ Ⓒ Ⓓ   4 Ⓐ Ⓑ Ⓒ Ⓓ   7 Ⓐ Ⓑ Ⓒ Ⓓ   10 Ⓐ Ⓑ Ⓒ Ⓓ

2 Ⓐ Ⓑ Ⓒ Ⓓ   5 Ⓐ Ⓑ Ⓒ Ⓓ   8 Ⓐ Ⓑ Ⓒ Ⓓ   11 Ⓐ Ⓑ Ⓒ Ⓓ

3 Ⓐ Ⓑ Ⓒ Ⓓ   6 Ⓐ Ⓑ Ⓒ Ⓓ   9 Ⓐ Ⓑ Ⓒ Ⓓ   12 Ⓐ Ⓑ Ⓒ Ⓓ

Go to the next page

C READING: "Help Wanted" Sign

Read the sign. Then answer the questions.

NOW HIRING!

- Looking for new employees.
- Days or eves
- FT & PT
- $13.00 / hr.
  Ask cashier in store for application form
---

13. What's the salary?
- Ⓐ Thirteen dollars per week.
- Ⓑ Thirteen dollars per month.
- Ⓒ Thirteen dollars per hour.
- Ⓓ Thirteen dollars per year.

14. What kind of jobs are there?
- Ⓐ Only jobs during the day.
- Ⓑ Only jobs during the evening.
- Ⓒ Only jobs for cashiers.
- Ⓓ Full-time jobs and part-time jobs.

15. What does a person have to do to apply for a job there?
- Ⓐ Fill out an application form.
- Ⓑ Work days and evenings.
- Ⓒ Look for new employees.
- Ⓓ Talk with the president of the company.

D READING: Classified Ads

Read the job advertisements. Then answer the questions.

HELP WANTED
BAKER
Small bakery. M–F. Full-time. Apply in person. G&R Pastry Shop. 700 Central Ave.
Secretary
Large office. Call Mary at 262-7910.
CASHIERS
Large supermarket. FT & PT. Days & eves. 420 Main St. Apply in person. Ask for Ray.

16. Chet can type and file. He's applying for a job. What does he have to do?
- Ⓐ He has to go to 700 Central Avenue.
- Ⓑ He has to go to 420 Main Street.
- Ⓒ He has to talk with Ray.
- Ⓓ He has to call 262-7910.

17. Sheila can use a cash register. She's applying for a job. What does she have to do?
- Ⓐ She has to work full-time.
- Ⓑ She has to go to 420 Main Street.
- Ⓒ She has to call Mary.
- Ⓓ She has to work part-time.

E LISTENING ASSESSMENT

Read and listen to the questions. Then listen to the job interview, and answer the questions.

18. Where is the job interview taking place?
- Ⓐ In a restaurant.
- Ⓑ In a bank.
- Ⓒ In a store.
- Ⓓ In a computer company.

19. What can David do?
- Ⓐ He can paint.
- Ⓑ He can take inventory.
- Ⓒ He can teach.
- Ⓓ He can use tools.

20. David doesn't have one skill. What <u>can't</u> he do?
- Ⓐ Take inventory.
- Ⓑ Use a cash register.
- Ⓒ Talk to customers.
- Ⓓ Operate business software.

. . . .

13 Ⓐ Ⓑ Ⓒ Ⓓ   15 Ⓐ Ⓑ Ⓒ Ⓓ   17 Ⓐ Ⓑ Ⓒ Ⓓ   19 Ⓐ Ⓑ Ⓒ Ⓓ

14 Ⓐ Ⓑ Ⓒ Ⓓ   16 Ⓐ Ⓑ Ⓒ Ⓓ   18 Ⓐ Ⓑ Ⓒ Ⓓ   20 Ⓐ Ⓑ Ⓒ Ⓓ

Go to the next page ⟩

Name _____ Date _____

Complete this form about yourself.

Name: _____ Social Security No. _____

Street: _____ Apartment: _____

City: _____ State: _____ Zip Code: _____

Telephone: _____

Skills and Abilities:

What can you do? Describe your skills and abilities:

_____

_____

_____

Work Experience:

Job	Company	From	To
_____	_____	____	____
_____	_____	____	____
_____	_____	____	____
_____	_____	____	____

Education:

School	City, State	From	To
_____	_____	____	____
_____	_____	____	____
_____	_____	____	____
_____	_____	____	____

Date: _____ Signature: _____

G POLICE/SAFETY COMMANDS & SIGNS

For each command, choose the correct sign.

1. "Danger! Don't stand there!" _____
2. "Danger! Don't touch that!" _____
3. "Wear a helmet!" _____
4. "Wear safety glasses!" _____
5. "Don't go that way!" _____
6. "Halt! Freeze! Don't move!" _____

H SPEAKING ASSESSMENT

I can ask and answer these questions about job skills and other abilities:

Ask Answer
☐ ☐ Can you ___job skill___?
☐ ☐ What can you do? Tell me about your skills.

☐ ☐ Can you play ___sport___?
☐ ☐ What sports can you play?

☐ ☐ Can you play ___musical instrument___?
☐ ☐ What musical instrument can you play?

Ask Answer
☐ ☐ Can you speak ___language___?
☐ ☐ What languages can you speak?

☐ ☐ Can you cook?
☐ ☐ What can you cook?

STOP

A TIME

1. It's _____.
- Ⓐ 7:00
- Ⓑ 8:00
- Ⓒ 6:30
- Ⓓ 7:30

5. What's the weather forecast for tomorrow?
- Ⓐ It rains.
- Ⓑ It's raining.
- Ⓒ It's going to rain.
- Ⓓ I'm going to go to the beach.

2. It's _____.
- Ⓐ 11:15
- Ⓑ 11:45
- Ⓒ 9:00
- Ⓓ 9:45

6. What are you going to do tomorrow?
- Ⓐ We're going to clean our apartment.
- Ⓑ He's going to cook.
- Ⓒ It's going to be cloudy.
- Ⓓ They're going to have a picnic.

3. It's _____.
- Ⓐ a quarter to five
- Ⓑ half past six
- Ⓒ half past five
- Ⓓ a quarter to six

7. What time does the train leave?
- Ⓐ It begins at 6:00.
- Ⓑ It's 6:00.
- Ⓒ It's going to leave.
- Ⓓ At 6:00.

4. The time is _____.
- Ⓐ a quarter to three
- Ⓑ a quarter to four
- Ⓒ half past three
- Ⓓ half past four

8. What's the date?
- Ⓐ It's 4:00.
- Ⓑ It's Thursday.
- Ⓒ It's April 10th.
- Ⓓ It's spring.

B GRAMMAR IN CONTEXT: Asking & Telling Time • Congratulating

9. _____ is it?
- Ⓐ What time
- Ⓑ What's the time
- Ⓒ Tell the time
- Ⓓ Tell me the time

10. _____
- Ⓐ It's sunny and warm.
- Ⓑ It's two o'clock.
- Ⓒ I'm going to study.
- Ⓓ It's November 4th.

11. _____ August 31st. Today is my birthday!
- Ⓐ Today
- Ⓑ It
- Ⓒ It's
- Ⓓ I'm

12. Congratulations! _____
- Ⓐ Oh no!
- Ⓑ Happy New Year!
- Ⓒ Happy Thanksgiving!
- Ⓓ Happy Birthday!

1 Ⓐ Ⓑ Ⓒ Ⓓ   4 Ⓐ Ⓑ Ⓒ Ⓓ   7 Ⓐ Ⓑ Ⓒ Ⓓ   10 Ⓐ Ⓑ Ⓒ Ⓓ

2 Ⓐ Ⓑ Ⓒ Ⓓ   5 Ⓐ Ⓑ Ⓒ Ⓓ   8 Ⓐ Ⓑ Ⓒ Ⓓ   11 Ⓐ Ⓑ Ⓒ Ⓓ

3 Ⓐ Ⓑ Ⓒ Ⓓ   6 Ⓐ Ⓑ Ⓒ Ⓓ   9 Ⓐ Ⓑ Ⓒ Ⓓ   12 Ⓐ Ⓑ Ⓒ Ⓓ

Go to the next page

C READING: National Holidays in the United States & Canada

Read the story. Then answer the questions.

> Some holidays in the United States and Canada are on the same date every year. New Year's Day is always on January 1st. Christmas Day is always on December 25th. Canadians always celebrate Canada Day on July 1st, and people in the United States always celebrate Independence Day on July 4th. Veterans Day in the U.S. and Remembrance Day in Canada are always on November 11th.
>
> Other holidays are on different dates every year because these holidays are on certain days of the week. For example, in the U.S. and Canada, Labor Day is always on the first Monday in September. Thanksgiving Day in the U.S. is always on the fourth Thursday in November. In Canada, Thanksgiving Day is on the second Monday in October. Many other U.S. holidays are always on Monday: Martin Luther King, Jr. Day in January, Presidents' Day in February, Memorial Day in May, and Columbus Day in October.

13. Which holiday is in September?

  Ⓐ Presidents' Day.
  Ⓑ Memorial Day.
  Ⓒ Columbus Day.
  Ⓓ Labor Day.

14. Which holiday is always on the same date every year?

  Ⓐ Thanksgiving Day.
  Ⓑ Labor Day.
  Ⓒ New Year's Day.
  Ⓓ Memorial Day.

15. Which sentence is correct?

  Ⓐ New Year's Day is always on Monday.
  Ⓑ Memorial Day in the U.S. is always on Monday.
  Ⓒ Canada Day is in June.
  Ⓓ Christmas Day is on December 24th.

16. Which sentence is <u>not</u> correct?

  Ⓐ Canada and the U.S. celebrate Labor Day on the same day.
  Ⓑ Canada and the U.S. have a holiday on November 11th.
  Ⓒ New Year's Day is on the first day of January.
  Ⓓ Canada and the U.S. celebrate Thanksgiving on the same day.

D LISTENING ASSESSMENT

Read and listen to the questions. Then listen to the story, and answer the questions.

17. What's he going to do in March?

  Ⓐ He's going to start a new job.
  Ⓑ He's going to move.
  Ⓒ He's going to get married.
  Ⓓ He's going to have a birthday party.

18. When is he going to begin to study at a computer school?

  Ⓐ In January.
  Ⓑ In June.
  Ⓒ In September.
  Ⓓ In December.

19. Where is he going to work?

  Ⓐ In an office.
  Ⓑ In a new apartment building.
  Ⓒ In a computer school.
  Ⓓ In Honolulu.

20. How old is he going to be in June?

  Ⓐ 13 years old.
  Ⓑ 23 years old.
  Ⓒ 30 years old.
  Ⓓ 40 years old.

13 Ⓐ Ⓑ Ⓒ Ⓓ   16 Ⓐ Ⓑ Ⓒ Ⓓ   19 Ⓐ Ⓑ Ⓒ Ⓓ

14 Ⓐ Ⓑ Ⓒ Ⓓ   17 Ⓐ Ⓑ Ⓒ Ⓓ   20 Ⓐ Ⓑ Ⓒ Ⓓ

15 Ⓐ Ⓑ Ⓒ Ⓓ   18 Ⓐ Ⓑ Ⓒ Ⓓ   Go to the next page ➡

E THE CALENDAR

2025

January	February	March	April
S M T W T F S	S M T W T F S	S M T W T F S	S M T W T F S
1 2 3 4	1	1	1 2 3 4 5
5 6 7 8 9 10 11	2 3 4 5 6 7 8	2 3 4 5 6 7 8	6 7 8 9 10 11 12
12 13 14 15 16 17 18	9 10 11 12 13 14 15	9 10 11 12 13 14 15	13 14 15 16 17 18 19
19 20 21 22 23 24 25	16 17 18 19 20 21 22	16 17 18 19 20 21 22	20 21 22 23 24 25 26
26 27 28 29 30 31	23 24 25 26 27 28	23/30 24/31 25 26 27 28 29	27 28 29 30

May	June	July	August
S M T W T F S	S M T W T F S	S M T W T F S	S M T W T F S
1 2 3	1 2 3 4 5 6 7	1 2 3 4 5	1 2
4 5 6 7 8 9 10	8 9 10 11 12 13 14	6 7 8 9 10 11 12	3 4 5 6 7 8 9
11 12 13 14 15 16 17	15 16 17 18 19 20 21	13 14 15 16 17 18 19	10 11 12 13 14 15 16
18 19 20 21 22 23 24	22 23 24 25 26 27 28	20 21 22 23 24 25 26	17 18 19 20 21 22 23
25 26 27 28 29 30 31	29 30	27 28 29 30 31	24/31 25 26 27 28 29 30

September	October	November	December
S M T W T F S	S M T W T F S	S M T W T F S	S M T W T F S
1 2 3 4 5 6	1 2 3 4	1	1 2 3 4 5 6
7 8 9 10 11 12 13	5 6 7 8 9 10 11	2 3 4 5 6 7 8	7 8 9 10 11 12 13
14 15 16 17 18 19 20	12 13 14 15 16 17 18	9 10 11 12 13 14 15	14 15 16 17 18 19 20
21 22 23 24 25 26 27	19 20 21 22 23 24 25	16/30 17 18 19 20 21 22	21 22 23 24 25 26 27
28 29 30	26 27 28 29 30 31	23 24 25 26 27 28 29	28 29 30 31

Circle these dates on the calendar.

March 7   June 2nd
September 25   5/13/25
April 15th   8/20/25
January 23rd   10/31/25

On this calendar, what day of the week is . . .

July 4th _____Friday_____   11/16/25 _____

February 10th _____   1/14/25 _____

May 22nd _____   3/5/25 _____

F ORDINAL NUMBERS

1st	11th	21st
2nd	12th	22nd
3rd	13th	23rd
4th	14th	24th
5th	15th	25th
6th	16th	26th
7th	17th	27th
8th	18th	28th
9th	19th	29th
10th	20th	30th

Write the correct ordinal number.

third _____   seventh _____

fifteenth _____   twenty-first _____

second _____   twelfth _____

thirtieth _____   eighteenth _____

G WRITING ASSESSMENT: Months of the Year

Look at the abbreviation. Write the correct month of the year.

MAR _____   DEC _____   APR _____

AUG _____   FEB _____   JUN _____

NOV _____   JAN _____   MAY _____

SEP _____   OCT _____   JUL _____

H CLOCK TIMES

_____*2:00*_____ _____ _____ _____ _____

I WRITING ASSESSMENT: Fill Out the Forms

First Name: _____   Last Name: _____

Date of Birth: _____   Place of Birth: _____

Signature: _____   Today's Date: _____

Last Name: | | | | | | | | | | | | | First Name: | | | | | | | | | | | | |

Date of Birth: | | | | | | | Today's Date: | | | | | | | Signature: [   ]
　　　　　　　Month Day Year　　　　　　　Month Day Year

J WRITING ASSESSMENT: Day & Date

What day is it? ....

What's today's date? ....

K WRITING ASSESSMENT: Future Plans

What are you going to do tomorrow? Tell about five or more things you are going to do. Use a separate sheet of paper.

L SPEAKING ASSESSMENT

I can ask and answer questions about dates, time, and weather:

Ask Answer
☐ ☐ What day is it today?
☐ ☐ What's today's date?
　　 What's the date
　　　today?

Ask Answer
☐ ☐ What day is it tomorrow?
☐ ☐ What's tomorrow's date?

Ask Answer
☐ ☐ What time is it?
☐ ☐ What's your birthdate?
☐ ☐ What's the weather forecast
　　　for tomorrow?

I can ask and answer questions about common activities and time:

Ask Answer
What time do you usually . . .
☐ ☐ get up?
☐ ☐ eat breakfast?
☐ ☐ go to school?
☐ ☐ eat lunch?
☐ ☐ eat dinner?
☐ ☐ go to bed?

Ask Answer
What time are you going to . . .
☐ ☐ get up tomorrow?
☐ ☐ eat breakfast tomorrow?
☐ ☐ go to school tomorrow?
☐ ☐ eat lunch tomorrow?
☐ ☐ eat dinner tomorrow?
☐ ☐ go to bed tomorrow?

STOP

A MEDICAL CARE: Parts of the Body & Ailments

Choose the correct answer.

Example:

Her _____ hurts. She has _____.
- Ⓐ throat . . a sore throat
- Ⓑ ear . . an earache
- ● head . . a headache
- Ⓓ tooth . . a toothache

1. Her _____ hurts. She has _____.
- Ⓐ back . . a backache
- Ⓑ ear . . an earache
- Ⓒ stomach . . a stomachache
- Ⓓ throat . . a sore throat

2. He has _____. He wants some _____.
- Ⓐ a fever . . cold
- Ⓑ a toothache . . candy
- Ⓒ a cold . . hot dogs
- Ⓓ cold . . cold medicine

3. He has _____. He wants some _____.
- Ⓐ a cough . . cough syrup
- Ⓑ a stomachache . . antacid tablets
- Ⓒ an earache . . ear drops
- Ⓓ a headache . . aspirin

4. Betsy has a stomachache because she _____ all day yesterday.
- Ⓐ eats cookies
- Ⓑ ate cookies
- Ⓒ rests
- Ⓓ rested

5. Robert has a backache because he _____ all day.
- Ⓐ talked
- Ⓑ sang
- Ⓒ planted flowers
- Ⓓ cried

6. Peggy has a sore throat because she _____ all day.
- Ⓐ shouted
- Ⓑ listened to loud music
- Ⓒ rode her bike
- Ⓓ studied

7. Carl called the _____ because he has _____.
- Ⓐ doctor's office . . a fever
- Ⓑ doctor's office . . a toothache
- Ⓒ dentist's office . . a fever
- Ⓓ dentist's office . . a toothache

1 Ⓐ Ⓑ Ⓒ Ⓓ   3 Ⓐ Ⓑ Ⓒ Ⓓ   5 Ⓐ Ⓑ Ⓒ Ⓓ   7 Ⓐ Ⓑ Ⓒ Ⓓ

2 Ⓐ Ⓑ Ⓒ Ⓓ   4 Ⓐ Ⓑ Ⓒ Ⓓ   6 Ⓐ Ⓑ Ⓒ Ⓓ

Go to the next page ▷

GRAMMAR IN CONTEXT: Calling for Medical Appointments & Emergency Assistance

Choose the correct answer to complete the conversation.

Example:
_____ Doctor Carter, please?
- Ⓐ Are you
- Ⓑ This is
- Ⓒ May you speak with
- ● May I speak with

8. _____
- Ⓐ Who's calling?
- Ⓑ Who called?
- Ⓒ Who do you call?
- Ⓓ How do you feel?

9. _____ Ted Rogers. I have a terrible backache.
- Ⓐ You are
- Ⓑ He's
- Ⓒ This is
- Ⓓ Hello

10. I'm _____ to hear that.
- Ⓐ glad
- Ⓑ fine
- Ⓒ okay
- Ⓓ sorry

11. Can I _____?
- Ⓐ seem to be the problem
- Ⓑ make an appointment
- Ⓒ feel fine
- Ⓓ what's the matter

12. Yes. Please _____ tomorrow at 2:00.
- Ⓐ hear that
- Ⓑ feel okay
- Ⓒ come in
- Ⓓ get it

13. This is an emergency! My grandfather _____!
- Ⓐ is very tired
- Ⓑ has a cold
- Ⓒ is very sick
- Ⓓ has a toothache

14. _____
- Ⓐ How does he feel today?
- Ⓑ How did he get it?
- Ⓒ Can you come in next Thursday?
- Ⓓ What's the matter?

15. I don't know. He ate dinner, and now he feels _____. And he can't talk.
- Ⓐ sorry
- Ⓑ so-so
- Ⓒ terrible
- Ⓓ not so good

Okay. An ambulance is on the way.

8 Ⓐ Ⓑ Ⓒ Ⓓ   10 Ⓐ Ⓑ Ⓒ Ⓓ   12 Ⓐ Ⓑ Ⓒ Ⓓ   14 Ⓐ Ⓑ Ⓒ Ⓓ

9 Ⓐ Ⓑ Ⓒ Ⓓ   11 Ⓐ Ⓑ Ⓒ Ⓓ   13 Ⓐ Ⓑ Ⓒ Ⓓ   15 Ⓐ Ⓑ Ⓒ Ⓓ

Go to the next page

C READING: Over-the-Counter Medications

Read the drug store directory. Choose the correct answer to complete each conversation.

DISCOUNT MEDICAL PHARMACY
STORE DIRECTORY

	Aisle
ASPIRIN	1
COUGH SYRUP	2
EAR DROPS	3
COLD MEDICINE	4
THROAT LOZENGES	5
ANTACID TABLETS	6

Can you help me? I need something for a sore throat.

16. Look in _____.
- Ⓐ Aisle 1
- Ⓑ Aisle 2
- Ⓒ Aisle 5
- Ⓓ Aisle 6

Excuse me. Do you have aspirin and other medicine for a headache?

17. Yes. Look in _____.
- Ⓐ Aisle 1
- Ⓑ Aisle 3
- Ⓒ Aisle 4
- Ⓓ Aisle 6

Excuse me. I'm looking for medicine for a stomachache.

18. _____
- Ⓐ Ear drops are in Aisle 3.
- Ⓑ Antacid tablets are in Aisle 6.
- Ⓒ Throat lozenges are in Aisle 5.
- Ⓓ Cold medicine is in Aisle 4.

D LISTENING ASSESSMENT

Read and listen to the questions. Then listen to the conversation at the drug store, and answer the questions.

19. What's the matter with the person?
- Ⓐ She can't hear that.
- Ⓑ She sings on the weekend.
- Ⓒ She's in Aisle Two.
- Ⓓ She has a sore throat.

20. What's she going to buy?
- Ⓐ Cough syrup.
- Ⓑ Throat lozenges.
- Ⓒ Cough syrup and throat lozenges.
- Ⓓ Cold medicine.

16 Ⓐ Ⓑ Ⓒ Ⓓ   18 Ⓐ Ⓑ Ⓒ Ⓓ   20 Ⓐ Ⓑ Ⓒ Ⓓ

17 Ⓐ Ⓑ Ⓒ Ⓓ   19 Ⓐ Ⓑ Ⓒ Ⓓ

Go to the next page ⟩

E DRUG LABELS, DOSAGES, & FILLING/REFILLING PRESCRIPTIONS

For each conversation in the drug store, choose the correct medicine.

tsp. = teaspoon	1x / day = once a day
tab. = tablet	2x / day = twice a day
cap. = capsule	3x / day = 3 times a day

A.   B.   C.   D.   E.

Example:

__C__   Take one pill twice a day.   One pill twice a day? Okay.

1. ____ Take two capsules four times a day.   I understand. Thank you.

2. ____ Do you understand the directions on the label?   Yes. I can take two capsules twice a day.

3. ____ Can you fill my prescription for cough syrup?   Yes. Please give me the prescription and take a seat. It's going to be about 20 minutes.

4. ____ Can I refill my prescription for these tablets?   Yes. You can refill this prescription one more time.

F INTERPRETING A FAHRENHEIT THERMOMETER & A DOSAGE CUP

Fill in the thermometer to show a normal body temperature of 98.6° F. (98.6 degrees Fahrenheit).

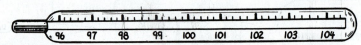

For each drug label, fill in the correct amount of medicine in the dosage cup.

G WRITING ASSESSMENT

Write about your dinner yesterday (or another day). What did you eat? Where? Who cooked the dinner? Who ate with you? Who washed the dishes? Write about it on a separate sheet of paper.

H SPEAKING ASSESSMENT

I can ask and answer these questions:

Ask Answer
☐ ☐ How do you feel today?
☐ ☐ What did you do yesterday?
☐ ☐ What did you eat yesterday?
☐ ☐ What did you drink yesterday?

STOP

A   COMMON ACTIVITIES IN THE PAST

Choose the correct answer.

Example:

My friends and I _____ a movie last Saturday.
- Ⓐ see
- Ⓑ did see
- Ⓒ saw
- Ⓓ did saw   Ⓐ Ⓑ ● Ⓓ

1. He _____ a book yesterday.
   - Ⓐ rode
   - Ⓑ red
   - Ⓒ did read
   - Ⓓ read

2. I _____ a bath yesterday evening. I usually _____ a shower.
   - Ⓐ took . . took
   - Ⓑ took . . take
   - Ⓒ take . . took
   - Ⓓ take . . take

3. I usually _____ dinner for my family, but yesterday my children _____ dinner.
   - Ⓐ make . . make
   - Ⓑ made . . make
   - Ⓒ make . . made
   - Ⓓ made . . made

4. _____ lunch yesterday?
   - Ⓐ Did she eat
   - Ⓑ Did she ate
   - Ⓒ She eat
   - Ⓓ She ate

5. _____ to work today?
   - Ⓐ Ms. Clark did drive
   - Ⓑ Ms. Clark drove
   - Ⓒ Did Ms. Clark drive
   - Ⓓ Did Ms. Clark drove

6. _____ his homework last night?
   - Ⓐ Did your brother
   - Ⓑ Did your brother did
   - Ⓒ Did your brother do
   - Ⓓ Do your brother did

7. What time _____ this morning?
   - Ⓐ you got up
   - Ⓑ you did get up
   - Ⓒ got up you
   - Ⓓ did you get up

8. _____ to school yesterday?
   - Ⓐ How do they go
   - Ⓑ How they do go
   - Ⓒ How did they go
   - Ⓓ How they did go

9. _____ at the supermarket?
   - Ⓐ What did they buy
   - Ⓑ What they buy
   - Ⓒ What did they bought
   - Ⓓ What they bought

10. Did you have a big breakfast today?
    - Ⓐ Yes, I do.
    - Ⓑ No, I don't.
    - Ⓒ Yes, they did.
    - Ⓓ No, I didn't.

11. Do you and your sister go to school every day?
    - Ⓐ Yes, she does.
    - Ⓑ Yes, we do.
    - Ⓒ Yes, she did.
    - Ⓓ Yes, we did.

1 Ⓐ Ⓑ Ⓒ Ⓓ   4 Ⓐ Ⓑ Ⓒ Ⓓ   7 Ⓐ Ⓑ Ⓒ Ⓓ   10 Ⓐ Ⓑ Ⓒ Ⓓ

2 Ⓐ Ⓑ Ⓒ Ⓓ   5 Ⓐ Ⓑ Ⓒ Ⓓ   8 Ⓐ Ⓑ Ⓒ Ⓓ   11 Ⓐ Ⓑ Ⓒ Ⓓ

3 Ⓐ Ⓑ Ⓒ Ⓓ   6 Ⓐ Ⓑ Ⓒ Ⓓ   9 Ⓐ Ⓑ Ⓒ Ⓓ

Go to the next page ⟩

B GRAMMAR IN CONTEXT: Apologizing for Lateness at Work

Choose the correct answer to complete the conversation.

Example:

_____ I'm late.
- (A) You're sorry
- (●) I'm sorry
- (C) He's sorry
- (D) She's sorry

12. _____
- (A) What's going to happen?
- (B) What's happening?
- (C) What happened?
- (D) What happens?

13. I _____ late and I _____ the bus.
- (A) get up . . miss
- (B) did get up . . did miss
- (C) got up . . miss
- (D) got up . . missed

14. _____
- (A) You understand.
- (B) I see.
- (C) You're sorry.
- (D) I have good excuses.

C READING: Safety Procedures

Read the safety posters. Then answer the questions on the next page.

Duck, Cover, & Hold!

What to Do At School During an Earthquake

IN A CLASSROOM:

Duck! Get down under a desk or table. (Don't go near windows, bookcases, or other tall furniture.)

Cover! Cover your head with the desk or table. Cover your eyes. (Put your face into your arm.)

Hold! Hold on to the desk or table so it stays over your head. (Furniture can move during an earthquake.)

IN THE HALL:

Drop! Sit on the floor near an inside wall. Get down on your knees. Lean over to rest on your elbows. Put your hands together behind your neck. Put your face down.

OUTSIDE:

Don't go near buildings or walls. Sit down, or use the "Drop" position.

Stop, Drop, Cover, & Roll!

What to Do If Your Clothing Is on Fire

Stop! Stop where you are. Don't run.

Drop! Drop to the ground.

Cover! Cover your face.

Roll! Roll from side to side, over and over, until the fire goes out.

15. Mr. Gardner's English class had an earthquake drill in their classroom today. What did the students do first?
    - Ⓐ They covered their eyes.
    - Ⓑ They went near the windows.
    - Ⓒ They got down under their desks.
    - Ⓓ They moved the furniture.

16. What didn't the students do during the earthquake drill?
    - Ⓐ They didn't cover their heads.
    - Ⓑ They didn't hold on to their desks.
    - Ⓒ They didn't cover their eyes.
    - Ⓓ They didn't roll from side to side.

17. What did students in the hall do during the earthquake drill?
    - Ⓐ They went to their classrooms.
    - Ⓑ They went outside.
    - Ⓒ They sat down near an inside wall.
    - Ⓓ They rested on the floor.

18. Your clothing is on fire. What are you going to do?
    - Ⓐ Duck, cover, and hold.
    - Ⓑ Stop, drop, cover, and roll.
    - Ⓒ Cover my head with a desk or table.
    - Ⓓ Run to a window.

D LISTENING ASSESSMENT

Read and listen to the questions. Then listen to the story, and answer the questions.

19. Which meals did she have yesterday?
    - Ⓐ She had breakfast and dinner.
    - Ⓑ She had lunch and dinner.
    - Ⓒ She had breakfast and lunch.
    - Ⓓ She had breakfast, lunch, and dinner.

20. What did she do at the mall?
    - Ⓐ She met her friend Bob.
    - Ⓑ She met her mother.
    - Ⓒ She ate lunch.
    - Ⓓ She bought a gift.

E WRITING & GRAMMAR ASSESSMENT

Example:

Did your parents wash their windows today?

No, they didn't.

They washed their car.

2. Did Mr. Lee drive a taxi today?

1. Did Sally go to the doctor this afternoon?

3. Did the students take the train to the zoo?

F EYE CONTACT & GESTURES

For each sentence, choose the correct picture.

A

B

C

D

E

F

1. "I understand." _____

2. "I don't understand." _____

3. "I'm happy to meet you." _____

4. "I have a question." _____

5. "I'd like to introduce my friend." _____

6. "I don't know." _____

G WRITING ASSESSMENT

What did you do yesterday? Write a paragraph about all the things you did. Use a separate sheet of paper.

H SPEAKING ASSESSMENT

I can ask and answer these questions about common activities (using full sentences):

Ask Answer

☐ ☐ What did you do yesterday?
☐ ☐ Did you study English yesterday?
☐ ☐ What time did you go to bed last night?
☐ ☐ What time did you get up today?
☐ ☐ Did you have breakfast this morning?
☐ ☐ What did you have for breakfast?
☐ ☐ How did you get to school today?
☐ ☐ What did you do last weekend?

STOP

A BASIC FOODS & COMMON CONTAINERS

1. Do you like _____?
Yes, I do.
- Ⓐ cookies
- Ⓑ pie
- Ⓒ spaghetti
- Ⓓ cake

2. Do you like _____?
No, I don't.
- Ⓐ cheese
- Ⓑ spaghetti
- Ⓒ cereal
- Ⓓ ice cream

3. Where are the _____?
They're over there.
- Ⓐ cake
- Ⓑ bread
- Ⓒ cookies
- Ⓓ cheese

4. What kind of _____ do you like?
I like apple _____.
- Ⓐ pie . . pie
- Ⓑ cake . . cake
- Ⓒ bread . . bread
- Ⓓ cookies . . cookies

5. What did you have for dessert?
We had a pint of _____.
- Ⓐ cookies
- Ⓑ ice cream
- Ⓒ soda
- Ⓓ milk

6. What did you buy at the supermarket?
We bought a loaf of _____.
- Ⓐ cheese
- Ⓑ cereal
- Ⓒ bread
- Ⓓ cake

7. What did they drink with their lunch?
They drank a bottle of _____.
- Ⓐ milk
- Ⓑ pie
- Ⓒ cheese
- Ⓓ soda

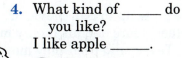

8. What did you buy at the grocery store?
I bought a gallon of _____.
- Ⓐ soda
- Ⓑ milk
- Ⓒ pie
- Ⓓ cereal

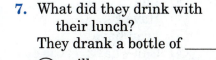

9. What did you get at the supermarket?
I got a pound of _____.
- Ⓐ cheese
- Ⓑ bread
- Ⓒ ice cream
- Ⓓ cereal

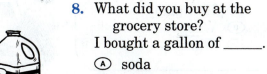

10. What do you want from the supermarket?
Please get a box of _____ for breakfast.
- Ⓐ milk
- Ⓑ cereal
- Ⓒ pie
- Ⓓ cheese

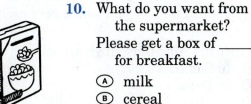

1 Ⓐ Ⓑ Ⓒ Ⓓ 3 Ⓐ Ⓑ Ⓒ Ⓓ 5 Ⓐ Ⓑ Ⓒ Ⓓ 7 Ⓐ Ⓑ Ⓒ Ⓓ 9 Ⓐ Ⓑ Ⓒ Ⓓ

2 Ⓐ Ⓑ Ⓒ Ⓓ 4 Ⓐ Ⓑ Ⓒ Ⓓ 6 Ⓐ Ⓑ Ⓒ Ⓓ 8 Ⓐ Ⓑ Ⓒ Ⓓ 10 Ⓐ Ⓑ Ⓒ Ⓓ

Go to the next page ⟩

B GRAMMAR IN CONTEXT: System of Weights Using Ounces & Pounds

Choose the correct answer to complete the conversation.

16 ounces = 1 pound (lb.)

11. How much is this _____?
- Ⓐ bread
- Ⓑ cake
- Ⓒ cheese
- Ⓓ pie

12. It's _____ per pound.
- Ⓐ ten cents
- Ⓑ ten dollars
- Ⓒ one dollar
- Ⓓ one hundred dollars

13. _____ half a pound, please?
- Ⓐ I have
- Ⓑ Have I
- Ⓒ I can have
- Ⓓ Can I have

14. _____ ounces? Okay.
- Ⓐ 4
- Ⓑ 8
- Ⓒ 12
- Ⓓ 16

15. _____ are the cookies? I want to buy two pounds.
- Ⓐ How much
- Ⓑ How many
- Ⓒ Who
- Ⓓ What

16. They're $6.00 per pound. That's going to be _____.
- Ⓐ $3.00
- Ⓑ $6.00
- Ⓒ $9.00
- Ⓓ $12.00

C READING

Read the story. Then answer the questions.

> Alex Fernandez was born in El Salvador. He grew up in San Salvador, the capital city of his country. When Alex was fourteen years old, his family moved to the United States. First they lived in Dallas, Texas, and then they moved to Miami, Florida. Alex began high school in Texas. He was sad when his family moved. He liked his high school in Dallas, and he had many friends there. But Alex was also very happy in his new high school. He met many new friends there. Alex finished high school last year. Now he works in a restaurant at the Miami airport, and he studies at a computer school at night. Next year, he's going to go to college in Tampa, Florida. Alex is looking forward to next year and a very exciting future.

17. Where did Alex finish high school?
- Ⓐ In San Salvador.
- Ⓑ In Dallas.
- Ⓒ In Miami.
- Ⓓ In Tampa.

18. Which sentence is <u>not</u> correct?
- Ⓐ Alex finished high school.
- Ⓑ Alex has a job.
- Ⓒ Alex goes to a computer school.
- Ⓓ Alex goes to college.

. . . .

11 Ⓐ Ⓑ Ⓒ Ⓓ   13 Ⓐ Ⓑ Ⓒ Ⓓ   15 Ⓐ Ⓑ Ⓒ Ⓓ   17 Ⓐ Ⓑ Ⓒ Ⓓ

12 Ⓐ Ⓑ Ⓒ Ⓓ   14 Ⓐ Ⓑ Ⓒ Ⓓ   16 Ⓐ Ⓑ Ⓒ Ⓓ   18 Ⓐ Ⓑ Ⓒ Ⓓ

Go to the next page ⟩

Name _____ Date _____

D LISTENING ASSESSMENT

Read and listen to the questions. Then listen to the commercial, and answer the questions.

19. What kind of product is this commercial about?
    - Ⓐ Shampoo.
    - Ⓑ Window cleaner.
    - Ⓒ Floor wax.
    - Ⓓ Vitamins

20. How did the person get the product?
    - Ⓐ Some friends gave the person the product.
    - Ⓑ The person got the product at a party.
    - Ⓒ The person got the product at a store.
    - Ⓓ The person got the product at work.

E FOOD ADS

Look at the advertisements for food. Answer the questions.

1. How much are two heads of lettuce? _____

2. What's the price of three oranges? _____

3. What's the price of six oranges? _____

4. How much is a pound of Swiss cheese? _____

5. How much is half a pound of Swiss cheese? _____

6. How much are two gallons of milk? _____

F CLOZE READING

Read the story and circle the correct words.

I Went to Bed Early

I go (went) did go   to bed early last night because I   was   were   am [1] very

tired. My sister   wasn't   didn't   not [2] go to bed early because she   has   have   had [3]

a lot of homework. She   did   do   does [4] her homework for two hours, and then she

go   goes   went [5] to bed.

G LEARNING SKILL: Categorizing

Write each word in the correct column.

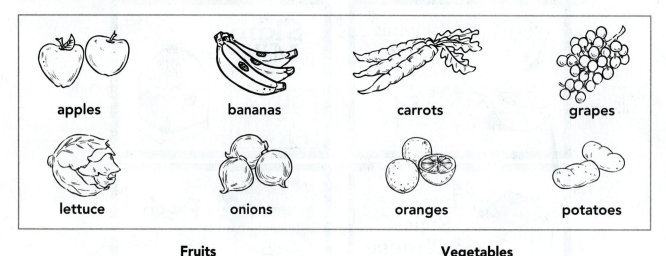

apples   bananas   carrots   grapes

lettuce   onions   oranges   potatoes

Fruits	Vegetables
apples	carrots
_____	_____
_____	_____
_____	_____

H WRITING ASSESSMENT

Write about your childhood. Where
were you born? Where did you
grow up? What did you look like?
Where did you go to school? What
did you do with your friends? (Use
a separate sheet of paper.)

I SPEAKING ASSESSMENT

I can ask and answer these questions:

Ask Answer
☐ ☐   What day was it yesterday?
☐ ☐   What was yesterday's date?
☐ ☐   Where were you yesterday?
☐ ☐   Where were you born?
☐ ☐   Where did you grow up?

STOP

SIDE by SIDE *Plus* Test Prep Workbook 1 Audio Program

The *Side by Side Plus Test Prep Workbook 1* Digital Audio CD contains all listening activities in the unit achievement tests. Teachers can choose to do these activities in class or have students complete them on their own using the audio. The Digital Audio CD also includes MP3 files of the audio program for downloading to a computer or audio player.

Track	Activity
1	Introduction
2	Unit 1: p. 3 Exercise E
3	Unit 2: p. 8 Exercise D
4	Unit 3: p. 10 Exercise C
5	Unit 4: p. 12 Exercise C
6	Unit 5: p. 14 Exercise D
7	Unit 6: p. 17 Exercise D
8	Unit 7: p. 21 Exercise D
9	Unit 8: p. 24 Exercise C
10	Unit 9: p. 30 Exercise C
11	Unit 10: p. 33 Exercise C
12	Unit 11: p. 36 Exercise C
13	Unit 12: p. 38 Exercise D
14	Unit 13: p. 40 Exercise E
15	Unit 14: p. 44 Exercise D
16	Unit 15: p. 49 Exercise D
17	Unit 16: p. 53 Exercise D
18	Unit 17: p. 57 Exercise D